Leading Empowerment

WITHDRAWN

Leading Empowerment

A practical guide to change

MICHAEL APPLEGARTH

Chandos Publishing
Oxford • England

Chandos Publishing (Oxford) Limited
Chandos House
5 & 6 Steadys Lane
Stanton Harcourt
Oxford OX29 5RL
UK
Tel: +44 (0) 1865 884447 Fax: +44 (0) 1865 884448
Email: info@chandospublishing.com
www.chandospublishing.com

First published in Great Britain in 2006

ISBN:
1 84334 143 3 (paperback)
1 84334 202 2 (hardback)

© M. Applegarth, 2006

Typeset by Domex e-Data Pvt. Ltd.
Printed in the UK and USA.

Contents

List of figures

Acknowledgements

Mike would like to thank his twin brother, Aidan, for his input and for sharing his up-to-date learning from his MBA at Warwick Business School. His insights into some cultural differences feature in the book from his experiences working for multinational corporations overseas.

And thanks too to Keith Posner at Positive Perspective, with whom Mike has worked on a number of leadership assignments and enjoyed much synergy.

About the author

Mike Applegarth began his vocation in training in 1979, having attained a Diploma in Business Studies. Following a few years within a manufacturing and sales environment, he then helped to establish a training consultancy for an insurance brokerage and this provided the trigger for acquiring the breadth of experience he now has of many different organisations, from the private and public sectors to charitable institutions. He has seen leadership and management in a wide range of industries such as insurance and finance, petrochemicals, pharmaceuticals, information technology and telecommunications, the tertiary sector, local government and public services.

His assignments as a consultant include the provision of executive coaching at senior management and director levels, the design and delivery of tailored leadership and management development programmes across all levels and functions of an organisation, the design and delivery of programmes covering communication and interpersonal skills, the research, design and delivery of tailored sales training solutions, and conducting training needs analyses and training audits.

Mike is involved, too, in developing company competence-based performance standards and in providing assessor training. In particular, he provided consultancy support and training for assessors for the national pilot of the Management Charter Initiative (MCI) Supervisor Level Standards. In addition, as an approved trainer for the

Institute of Leadership and Management (ILM), Mike conducts structured project-based programmes for clients seeking accreditation from the ILM.

Mike is also the author of the book *How to Take a Training Audit*, sponsored by Kogan Page in conjunction with the Institute of Training and Development (ITD), first published in July 1991. This addresses the best-practice approach to establishing a training function, and how its cost-effectiveness (or value for money) can be assessed. Further publications include *The Empowerment Pocketbook*, *The Project Management Pocketbook* and *The Call Centre Customer Care Pocketbook*, each of which he has co-authored in the Management Pocketbook series.

The author may be contacted at:

Applegarth Professional Training
Manfield House, Collins Gardens
Ash, Guildford
GU12 6EP

Tel: 01252 338517
E-mail: *mapple@globalnet.co.uk*

What is empowerment?

A definition

There is a good deal of confusion about 'empowerment' because it is a term that has seemingly been used in different contexts. From the 'empowerment of women' to boasts of an 'empowered workforce', it has been used as an expression that conveys strength, achievement of purpose and self-direction. Yet there is the suggestion that it is something you give to yourself, while at the same time it is something that is bestowed on you. Is it a management style? Is it an organisational culture? Is it merely a state of mind?!

We will explore its relevance to each of these in this book. The hint of 'power' perhaps gives the wrong impression, as it is not about devolving authority, though that may appear to be an outcome.

A look in the dictionary will generally provide two synonyms rather than the definition from a corporate perspective. It will cite 'authority' and 'power'.

However,

- *authority* – only exists with the presumption of subordinates, yet we cannot give employees authority over customers, for example;
- *power* – can be switched on or off.

Instead, the term or synonym which best describes empowerment is 'licence':

- *licence* – where the scope and conditions that apply are expressed, and where it is only issued after the licence-holder has proven their ability.

A useful analogy is the attainment of a car driver's licence:

- The licence empowers you to drive a car in your home country or even abroad, once your ability is proven.
- The conditions are not so restrictive that the car must be a specific model or that the route must always be the same.
- However, it does not empower you to drive a heavy goods vehicle (HGV) or a fire-engine for which separate licences are required.
- The Highway Code (in the UK) provides guidelines of acceptability with which every driver should be familiar.
- The outcomes are the same for all – arrival at our destinations safely.

So what would such a licence look like at work?

- It empowers employees to act within an organisational framework without frequent recourse to authority.
- Employees focus on outcomes and are not constrained by rigid controls – they are involved even at the planning stage.
- Authority may still need to be sought outside the scope of the empowerment or further development provided.
- Codes of practice, a statement of values or customer charters can still exist as core guidelines.
- Everyone has the freedom to achieve using their initiative.

From the leader's perspective, 'empowerment' is the mechanism by which we let the followers know what the destination will look like when they get themselves there.

The followers are no longer followers of a narrow directive issued on a task-by-task basis but followers of a broader vision. They can even participate in describing and clarifying the vision. More importantly, it is their skills and knowledge that ultimately gives them the power to deliver on it. They need to know that getting there won't happen by chance or accident, and that they won't be carried there. Instead, they will be given guidance and support to ensure the work they do will be effective in holding course for the intended destination.

The background

The term 'empowerment' was promulgated by Rosabeth Moss Kanter at Harvard Business School during the 1990s, where it had its origins within the context of sharing knowledge with employees through the advent of information technology (IT). After all, knowledge is power. Empowerment, however, is an evolutionary process, in much the same way as leadership is, and has begun to assume a greater significance for both the organisation and the individual. It is now identified with the knowledge that gives power and is achievable without recourse to IT. Indeed, the roots of empowerment as we know it today actually took hold to counter the negative social consequences of new technology.

Researchers at the Tavistock Institute in the UK first drew attention to the negative impact of new technology on worker productivity and satisfaction. In the 1950s both the coal-mining and textile-weaving industries saw the arrival of new technology clash with an established work ethic and social system, and this was continued during the 1970s in the car industry following the increased automation of assembly lines. Absenteeism, reduced productivity and even sabotage threatened sustainability. To combat this, the Scandinavian car manufacturers (Volvo and Saab) introduced the concept of autonomous work groups.

These work groups addressed the social needs of employees and provided a forum for participating in the introduction of new technology rather than be simply subjected to it. The workers organised themselves to carry out tasks towards their designated assignments and the impact on productivity was significant. A Volvo special-purpose plant achieved 100 per cent efficiency against only 80 per cent for its non-redesigned plants, while similar gains were being witnessed in work-group redesigns in both mining and weaving. Empowerment had released the collective – and often tacit – knowledge of the workforce for the common good. Those nearest to the task in hand took responsibility for accomplishing it, while management set the parameters and facilitated rather than dictated.

When applied correctly then, empowerment can become the vehicle for synergy and positive change as well as the attainment of team success through individual accomplishment. The individual and team relationship is an important context: individuals are motivated when the right buttons are pressed and demotivated when they are not. Since teams comprise individuals, the relative weighting of motivated to demotivated members will determine the impact of empowerment for the organisation as a whole, as we shall see later (Chapter 7).

'Empowering' therefore requires that the person being empowered has a clear picture of what their role looks like – or what key activities will look like – when it's done well, or not done well. As a leader you provide a vision, but don't fall into the trap of merely describing how something should be done – instead describe what the outcomes will look like when it's achieved. Support the latter and people have the opportunity to develop their skills and gain a sense of achievement: the former will only produce followers who can't think for themselves, or worse still, just think of leaving.

Perhaps it is no coincidence that 'empowerment' is a practice that has grown since the mid-1990s alongside performance standards (referred to in the UK as competences) used in the National Vocational Qualification (NVQ) framework. With the role of leader or manager recognised as an occupation, irrespective of the industry, as far back as the 1980s, there are now National Occupational Standards (NOS) for leaders and managers that were introduced in September 2005. What these have in common is a basis for expressing what outcomes look like, thus leading people to fulfil that vision.

Terminology

We will be seeing the term 'competence' later, so it is worth clarifying now its distinction from that word often confused with it, 'competency'. A 'competence' is a statement of an outcome that is achieved in a job, and it is the framework used in the UK for National Occupational Standards and National Vocational Qualifications. A 'competency', by contrast, is a description of the individual carrying out the job, and originates from an American approach to performance standards. It, however, describes input and often has degrees of competency, thus allowing or acknowledging variations in performance. Personally, I believe the best practice is to express the competences firstly, then only describe the competency that fits the achievement of those outcomes. Either people 'can' or they 'can't' do something – degrees of competency, or grey areas, create confusion and permit poor performance.

Correctly expressed outcomes describe the quality of an activity. Previously, all that managers had to measure themselves against were the quantitative indicators set out in business targets, on budget spreadsheets and in returns on investment. More often than not, they wouldn't have had agreement in setting them, nor could they always see the direct impact they had on such figures!

In fact, providing the focus on developing a true empowerment culture, by clarifying the scope of the licence given, providing the right 'tools' and developing the relevant skills, is a much more effective approach to ensuring the organisation is equipped to meet its objectives and business needs. Plans are for the future and so is development, but where's the future in just repeating today?

Where's the future in everyone on the road still being a learner, having to drive accompanied by an instructor and being restricted from the fast-track motorway? Once they have achieved the outcomes set in the driving test – thus showing that they have the skills and knowledge – they are given the licence to drive alone, going whichever routes they choose and choosing from a vast array of vehicles over which to take control. Yet everyone also knows what safe driving looks like and what the limitations of the licence are. They may, however, only know what safe driving looks like because they have a clear picture of what constitutes unsafe driving. We will see later the downfall of this approach. At least they will also know what to expect if the terms of the licence are breached.

Empowering can therefore follow the analogy of granting a driving licence but not acquiring a television licence. While each defines the scope and conditions that apply, there is no performance standard on how well you watch television. Perhaps with the government intervening in the UK on matters concerned with health and family values, such standards may not be far away!

Empowerment is permanent, unless the individual breaks the terms of the licence. It is not something to be switched on and off. Imagine the impact of the driving licence being terminated without an offence being committed. Imagine being given the licence but having no car to drive. Imagine having the car to drive but your boss always driving it for you. When we imagine, we see how things may look. 'What will it look like?' is a question every leader should be asking so they can choose the desired vision and clarify it for the team.

In the realms of 'personal development', empowerment is synonymous with 'transformation'. Yet again, though, the context of it implies that people transform themselves, having received the power to do so.

In these circumstances they are given permission to create their own vision and question themselves to explore the outcomes they desire. All they may then require are the tools, skills and knowledge to enable themselves – or perhaps simply the realisation that they already possess what they need. The power comes from within. Once switched on it has to remain on and not fall prey to circuit failure.

Being empowered is a choice that you make, and it is very much linked to how you see the world. Vision, yet again, is at the core.

Perceptions

At a workshop on 'Empowerment' in September 2005 the participants were women, all 35 of them, a mix of managers and team members. When asked to contribute their own perceptions initially on what empowerment might be defined as, the key words or phrases offered included:

- assertive
- control
- delegation
- enabled
- decisive
- confidence
- ownership
- self-awareness and choice
- ability to take charge of your own destiny
- self-belief
- freedom to make choices
- breaking down barriers
- having the tools to be able to do things
- freedom to do a bit extra
- others' belief in you.

As you can see there is quite a mixture of perceptions, yet every contribution bears the hallmark of a positive experience – or at least the anticipation of one. Each word or phrase also tried to capture what that individual had in mind, but we may still need to ask the questions: 'What does being assertive look like, sound like and feel like to you?' 'What does being in control look like, sound like and feel like to you?' And so on. Only by exploring further the more tangible descriptors can we really know whether we're relating to the same experiences or ambitions.

The more the tangibles were aired, the more able the group was to confer their agreement on what empowerment looks like, sounds like and feels like. The group had progressed from subjective assessment to objective expressions, such that others can make the same judgements as to whether those looks and sounds exist or not. It is easier to see the same things when you both know what you are looking for, or to hear the same thing when you both know what the words sound like.

Feelings by their very nature are subjective, though the discussion made it possible for the participants to describe them more objectively too. We can describe how a feeling makes us look or affects what we say (that others can hear) or how it affects what we do (that others can see). In the case of personal transformation perhaps we are not concerned with whether or not others can see or hear what empowerment feels like to us. All that matters is that we feel empowered.

The chances are though that our inner sense of empowerment does in fact make us look different and sound different to others as we feel more confident and certain about our actions.

The women at the workshop recognised that in the work environment you can't empower yourself without the approval of your manager or leader. It has to be a shared experience. They have to confirm that the scope you want to give yourself is within acceptable boundaries. Why? Well organisations have boundaries to give them structure, but it doesn't mean that they are set in concrete. Get agreement on how far the boundaries can be pushed but don't demolish them altogether.

Even the most desperate to be empowered recognise that there will inevitably be limits to the scope they are allowed. Unless it is already a function of their job they don't have burning desires to write and implement policy. They would like to be consulted though where it has an impact on them. Unless it is in their job description (or job profile) they don't want to determine organisational strategy for the next five years, though they would like to be heard if they believe they have something to offer in that direction.

Doing the jobs of other people is not empowering unless they first have the freedom to do their own jobs without unnecessary constraint.

A particularly enlightening exercise was exploring the 'barriers to being empowered'. This produced the extensive list of responses given below:

- personal/family obligations
- not being comfortable in the work situation
- being offended when you get 'used' for specific skills
- demands of the role
- reduced hours = a reduced role
- certain people
- geographical location
- time of day/working hours
- being seen
- traditional management style of wanting to know about everything
- managers not letting go
- job titles and perceptions of what they mean
- people recruiting in their own image
- the old boy's network
- unfair fast-tracking

- succession planning for those whose faces fit
- perception that you have to have served your time to progress
- wondering what you are allowed to do at your level
- blame culture
- seeking approval
- line manager's confidence in you
- visibility – where you sit and with whom
- rules and regulations
- yourself – self-confidence
- fear of showing yourself up
- out of your comfort zone
- others seem more capable
- other people's views of you (or what you think their view of you is)
- different perceptions of what empowerment is.

These barriers appear to suggest the following:

- Empowerment is dependent upon individual personalities.
- We can generate our own barriers.
- Leaders and managers are the barriers.
- Personal circumstances have to be right.

We will see in later chapters, however, why the mechanisms of empowerment can remove such barriers, why performance and not personality becomes the focus, why it achieves 'enabling' rather than 'disabling' and, in particular, how leaders and managers can have more control and free up their own time.

For, while it is the workforce that is empowered, it is the leaders who do the empowering. To understand why empowerment is a key tool for leadership, we first need to recognise what true leadership looks like.

2

The role of leadership in empowerment

Leading in context

'Leadership' is most commonly referred to as 'providing the inspiration for people to achieve their best'. Leaders have a vision for the future, they go beyond the here and now and create a compelling image to unlock the potential of their employees as they rise to meet the collective challenge.

The Chinese philosopher Laotse (500 BC) has been accredited with the following quotes:

> A leader is best when people barely know he exists, not so good when people obey and acclaim him, worse when people despise him ...

> Fail to honour people, and they will fail to honour you ...

> Be a good leader who talks little, has done his work, fulfilled his aim, and they will say, 'We did it ourselves'.

Leadership is not dictatorship where empowerment is concerned. Nor is it a case of do it as I would do it. None of the great leaders ever did it all themselves. They enthused, they motivated, they instilled belief in their followers, and above all they kept communicating and restating the vision.

Perhaps the adage referred to in Chapter 1 should read 'knowledge of the vision is power' – after all, we can't see a thing when we're kept in the dark!

Contrary to the myth, leaders are made – not born. A survey conducted by the Chartered Management Institute (CMI) in January 2005 established a direct relationship between effective leadership and management development, leading to improved organisational performance. The evidence was accrued using archive data gathered in 1996, 2000 and 2004 to track changing patterns of leadership and management development policy and practice.

Leadership takes different forms. It can be the rousing 'body of a woman but stomach and heart of a King' vocal variety (Elizabeth I); the first-man-over-the-top-of-the-trenches action variety; or the 'we're all in the same boat but I've sailed before' passive collaboration variety. As with empowerment, the effectiveness of leadership is then contextual. Lead vocally when the team is looking for action and you're not leading at all.

Now we know what leadership is, let's look at its impact. And what better analogy to draw than to lead a ship!

Plain sailing?

If you were to lead a ship in a competitive race across 3,000 miles of ocean from one continent to another, what would you need? A full complement of able-bodied people who know the ropes so you can leave them to it? Or a willing and energetic crew to whom the rigging of the boat is an unexplored maze and your direction is necessary each time their input is required? Can you really be in so many places at the same time?!

What if you were fortunate enough to recruit the complement of able-bodied crew members: how certain are you that they would know the layout and workings of your ship, with each knowing who does what and when? Allowing for contingencies, what reaction would you want from them in an emergency?

So how should you lead your ship?

You should be creating a vision: a vision of success, a picture of what each role contributes and what efficiency and effectiveness will look like. You may even practise emergency procedures with them. But one thing is certain – if a crew member doesn't pull their weight or pulls in the wrong sail, you may find the entire ship is all at sea.

People follow leaders because they share the same vision of where they will end up. Yet, if that vision is not there what guarantee is there that they will arrive in the same place together, or even recognise the accomplishment when they get there?

Leadership drives the process through which a vision is transformed into action and realised.

This aptly called 'transformational approach' to leadership makes the link between the known present and the unknown future. It is at the root, for example, of sports psychology.

Sports psychologists get their clients to focus their minds on seeing what the success they seek looks like, sounds like and feels like. Giving the mind a full description of the task at hand allows it to form a plan to accomplish the goal. The sports person then gets the power from within to make the vision a reality. Empowerment applies similar thinking to achieving goals that others set. See the whole picture and you can commit entirely: in fact, you can lead yourself.

That expression probably says more about what being empowered feels like. We can lead ourselves towards a goal that has become ours. It may have originated as someone else's, but it is one we have the inner power to make happen.

Even the term 'empowerment' exudes something that is positive and drives itself. The picture that describes the desired outcomes should be focused on the positives, in just the same way as the sports psychologist would work on their client. My own experience of sport and of the mind in general is that the mind doesn't recognise the existence of 'don't'. Anyone who has ever stood on a golf tee and told themselves not to put the ball in the water or lose it in the trees will know what I mean. You can hit extraordinary shots and be extremely accurate simply because your mind took that visual thought and made it a reality – it just didn't hear the 'don't'! Yet by focusing on the fairway and nothing else it is possible to avoid the hazards. Just don't allow yourself that last momentary thought that you're focusing on the fairway because you don't want to go in the water!

We may have heard the term 'being in the zone', when sportsmen and sportswomen are so mentally attuned to the task in hand that everything seems possible and negativity has no place. Perhaps they could be referring to the 'empowerment zone' that we will see in the next chapter.

Empowerment leadership

In the late 1970s, the situational leadership model was developed by Blanchard and Hersey. It identified four phases of leadership, putting a positive spin on the appropriate leadership style for given situations (see Figure 2.1).

The matrix shows the correlation between focus on the task and giving attention to the leader's relationship with his or her team. The authors implied that task focus was the extent to which the leader 'interfered' in how the task was carried out.

Figure 2.1   The situational leadership model

		COACHING	SUPPORTING
High			
		Low task and high relationship	High task and high relationship
RELATIONSHIP BEHAVIOUR (SUPPORTIVE BEHAVIOUR)	2	3	
		DIRECTING	DELEGATING
		Low task and low relationship	High task and low relationship
Low	1	4	

High   Low
**TASK BEHAVIOUR
(DIRECTIVE BEHAVIOUR)**

Source: Blanchard and Hersey (1977).

Contrast that with the leader focusing instead on what the task will look like when it has been completed to the required standard – but without dictating how it is carried out. The relationship with the team develops by discussing and clarifying outcomes and ensuring that 'followers' have the foundation skills and knowledge to accomplish the task or activity.

We could therefore modify the situational leadership model to reflect where empowering is positioned as a leadership style (see Figure 2.2). It can only exist after enabling has taken place and where continued support is available for actions taken within the agreed scope of the follower's role.

Blanchard and Hersey labelled phase 2 as 'Coaching'. However, in our context it is just as important to provide the right tools and work materials in addition to the skills and knowledge; hence, we refer to 'enabling'. The empowering and supporting phase allows team members the responsibility and initiative to achieve the outcomes expected of them in their own role, without the need for constant referral or the fear of potential retribution.

Figure 2.2   The leading empowerment model

	ENABLING	EMPOWERING
High	Low initiative and high relationship	High initiative and high relationship
TWO-WAY INVOLVEMENT (SUPPORTIVE BEHAVIOUR)	**DIRECTING**	**DELEGATING**
Low	Low initiative and low relationship	High initiative and low relationship

High   Low

**INITIATIVE AND RESPONSIBILITY
(LETTING GO BEHAVIOUR)**

Adapted from: Blanchard and Hersey (1977).

What you expect of them should not be kept to yourself. In fact, why not apply job profiles, as shown in Chapter 5? These provide a focus on what the outcomes of a role look like and can be used throughout the staff cycle of recruit, retain and release.

Where does delegation fit in? The key distinction is that when you delegate it is part of your own job that you give away for others to do: the responsibility for carrying out the task is delegated while the accountability stays with you. You should only delegate to people who have been enabled to carry out the task and to whom you are able to offer support if necessary. Empowerment, on the other hand, is empowering individuals to do their own job and meet the expectations of their own roles, not yours.

But what of other terms attributed to leaders – transformational versus transactional for example?

While transformational leadership has its fans, it's not without its critics. It presupposes that the vision is correct and that therefore what the followers do is correct. It further assumes that all followers have the same, clear and unequivocal vision in their mind. As we shall see below, this isn't necessarily so.

Some models of leadership

Understanding leadership has been a primary goal of academics for the past half-century. Yet despite voluminous research, there is no consensus. The oft quoted 'leaders are born, not made' has now been rebutted by the Chartered Management Institute (CMI) survey in January 2005. Fielder et al. (1978) theorised that it is easier for a leader to try and change the situation than to change his style. This was contradicted by Vroom and Yetton in 1973, as well as by Blanchard and Hersey. They found that leaders should change their style to match situations. Who is right? Who is wrong? The simple answer is that neither is right and neither is wrong: they are half right and half wrong. Let's see why.

Context is the hidden denominator. In a military conflict when timely action may be critical, the normally authoritative leader who gets his group together for a participative discussion during a firefight may be considered by his troops to have 'lost it'. Just when they look to the leader for decisiveness, they get the opposite. A change in leadership style at this stage may not only be unexpected but wholly unwanted, losing the acceptance of the followers. Leaders chosen for a task because of the suitability of their character may find that a change in character means they are no longer up to the task. This would support Fielder.

On the other hand, under less critical conditions where a leader is, say, seeking to coax his team into designing and implementing a new marketing campaign, the leader may need to adapt to the differing requirements. To encourage the collective juices to flow freely during the formulating stage, a collaborative/consultative style would be more productive, facilitating discussion rather than dictating one's own views. Later, as the more time-challenged implementation gets underway, the leader may need to adopt a more autocratic approach in order to realise the vision on time. This would support Vroom and Yetton.

Thus we have two opposing perspectives, each supported by context.

It should come as no surprise then to learn that the more recent academic stance addresses a contextual approach to leadership.

The contextual approach

In short, the contextual approach sees leadership as a negotiated process worked out between leader, group and situation (Hosking, 1988). It's that simple.

People, processes and contexts become inextricably linked to any analysis of leadership. To anyone who has ever led or been led (and that must be all of us) it's an obvious finding, but what is not so obvious are the implications. For while Vroom and Yetton as well as Blanchard and Hersey have suggested that a leader need merely change his style to match a situation, it is clear that as individuals some leaders suit some situations better than others. For example, Winston Churchill's leadership was very much welcomed and respected during the crisis of the Second World War. Yet when it was peacetime he was no longer in vogue. Leadership then is not only contextual, it's individually selective.

The expression 'horses for courses' recognises that some horses are better suited to a firm ground while others perform best on heavy, wet soil. The dynamic autocrat often sought to kickstart or ruthlessly turn around a business is unlikely to become the collaborative facilitator needed once things stabilise. Even if he could achieve the personality shift, it's unlikely that he will be accepted by those same followers in a new guise, the one character being such a contrast to the other that it appears almost schizophrenic, the one set of traits seeming a betrayal of the other. No wonder then that we see a rotation of leaders in industry, brought in to realise the vision of the day.

Where does this all lead? To a realisation of the impact and destiny of leadership. For there are now recognised categories of leader.

Leavy and Wilson (1994: 113) identified four distinct roles for leaders:

1. *Builders* – those who typically have founded the organisation or who lead it in its formative stages.
2. *Revitalisers* – those who inject a new sense of purpose without altering the strategic direction of the firm.
3. *Turnarounders* – those whose influence changes the strategy, structure and often the direction of the firm.
4. *Inheritors* – those who see through the vision of their predecessors.

(Leavy and Wilson seem to have missed the 'Slashers': those whose sole purpose is to come in and undo whatever it was their predecessor did, just for the sake of it!)

Realising the vision

We will all know of someone – via our own experience or the media – who we can categorise by their reputation or past performance. But where do we see ourselves, and more importantly, where do others see us? For how we are perceived will impact on whether our vision is followed. To elaborate, here's a real-life example.

Following the 'merger' of two international banks in 1998, a new leader was appointed as Global Head for one of the combined product lines. He had no prior experience of the product but was politically well placed with the new hierarchy to support it. He saw himself as an inspirational leader. However, his appointment was viewed with scepticism by his new followers and far from trusting his new vision, they saw a hidden agenda. How could this be? Perhaps it was the fact that in his two prior assignments he had presided over the wind-down of businesses. He fell into that category of 'hatchet man', for which there is little empirical support but a wealth of conventional wisdom. When he envisioned growth, his followers saw decline. He said black, they saw white. Reservations were expressed about the leader's true mission, but each reassurance merely fuelled the embers of doubt. In the end, the leader did indeed preside over the wind-down of his new domain. Was it intentional? By all accounts yes.

So it's one thing to express a vision. It's quite another to see it realised. Ironically, it was the leader's hidden unspoken vision which was seen by the followers and which was ultimately transformed. Had they facilitated it? Perhaps, even though the decision to wind down was preconceived. But constantly addressing the threat of closure was certainly a distraction from achieving a more positive outcome.

Taking the contextual approach a stage further, there were other factors in the 'people, processes, situation' trilogy that had a bearing on the outcome, namely nationality and culture. The Anglo-Saxons were the most vociferous doubters, while the Asians seldom voiced disapproval and the diligent Swiss tended to accept what was being portrayed. The two merged institutions had the same nationality, but their cultures were opposing. In the context of this melee, what arose were opposing camps: the doubters, the believers and the neutrals. The authority was with the believers, but the power (to actually deliver on objectives) vested in the doubters. One culture accepted what it was told, the other openly debated it. Empowerment was not achieved because neither the people, the processes nor the situation were ever synchronised.

We could delve further into the leadership psyche. Aside from nationality and culture, research has even indicated that the gender of the leader makes a difference. Most studies on leadership have addressed a Western male dominance, some even arguing that women are too emotional to be fit to lead. That was then. Today, emotional intelligence is considered an advantage and unsurprisingly women comprise an increasing element of management in the workplace. Would the arrogant alpha male accept being led by a woman?

We don't wish to make any judgements here, but simply draw attention to the complexity of leadership. A leader who has the ability to inspire transformation in any given context is truly exceptional.

Empowerment though is not so much a role as a style and a state of mind. Any of the above roles could adopt it and the initial interaction that it engenders helps to achieve what only charisma could previously manage.

So what makes a good leader? Charisma has been frequently highlighted as the hallmark of an influential leader. It has become so important a factor that we now have a charismatic model of leadership (see Figure 2.3).

23

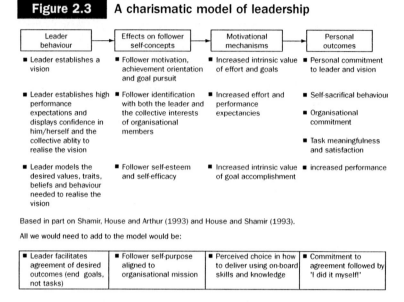

Figure 2.3 A charismatic model of leadership

Leader behaviour	Effects on follower self-concepts	Motivational mechanisms	Personal outcomes
■ Leader establishes a vision	■ Follower motivation, achievement orientation and goal pursuit	■ Increased intrinsic value of effort and goals	■ Personal commitment to leader and vision
■ Leader establishes high performance expectations and displays confidence in him/herself and the collective ablity to realise the vision	■ Follower identification with both the leader and the collective interests of organisational members	■ Increased effort and performance expectancies	■ Self-sacrifical behaviour ■ Organisational commitment ■ Task meaningfulness and satisfaction
■ Leader models the desired values, traits, beliefs and behaviour needed to realise the vision	■ Follower self-esteem and self-efficacy	■ Increased intrinsic value of goal accomplishment	■ increased performance

Based in part on Shamir, House and Arthur (1993) and House and Shamir (1993).

All we would need to add to the model would be:

■ Leader facilitates agreement of desired outcomes (end goals, not tasks)	■ Follower self-purpose aligned to organisational mission	■ Perceived choice in how to deliver using on-board skills and knowledge	■ Commitment to agreement followed by 'I did it myself!'

The model builds on the findings that, under charismatic leadership, followers:

■ trust the correctness of the leader's beliefs;

■ share similar beliefs;

■ accept the leader unquestionably;

■ feel affection for the leader;

■ obey the leader willingly;

■ are emotionally involved in the organisational mission;

■ have heightened performance goals; and

■ believe they can contribute to the success of the group's mission.

Such leadership provides the epitome of empowerment. Followers not only want to follow the vision but feel sufficiently emotionally linked to give their best performance and self-sacrifice to achieve it. All that needs adding to the model is shown below it.

Under the *empowering* style, followers may not feel affection for the leader and may not accept the leader unquestionably: the style allows for questions to be raised so that the follower can fully understand the desired outcomes and any constraints they have to work under.

Contrast this with so-called *transactional leadership*. This is characterised by task-orientated, uninspiring exchanges towards routine achievement, for which the follower has little emotion and limited aspiration to give of their best. This would be typical of a leader using a 'directing' style when a 'supporting' or empowering one was more appropriate. Followers would see this as interference. Which leadership style would you prefer to exhibit?

3

Exploring the need and the benefits

The need

The need for empowerment can be expressed again by the sailing analogy. The leader or skipper can't be awake every minute of the day and therefore needs to share with his crew his vision of where he expects to be when he's next on deck. More than giving a simple compass bearing though, he needs to share his knowledge of weather patterns, the whereabouts of other vessels, known hazards and the presence of way-points to enable his crew to use their own discretion during his absence. By now he should already take comfort that his crew are well able to run the ship to the next milestone without him ... after all, he will have ensured that trust when appointing the watch leaders.

The analogy needs little explanation. Leaders do not do everything themselves. They simply can't. The ship does not put to anchor just because the leader takes a nap. It sails on towards its objective in the hands of a competent crew that can tack or gybe its way round emerging obstacles always with the end goal in mind.

The conundrum that empowerment provides is that it grants freedom while using controls to achieve it. Empowerment does not mean less control – which represents the main objection to adopting it – but rather it allows for the controls imposed externally on the individual to be transferred internally to them. The outcomes are the controls and not the inputs, therefore the individual is allowed some autonomy in how they go about achieving those outcomes. They feel empowered – set free to do it their way, so long as ... They are in possession of the control, which is where it needs to be when they're doing the driving.

So if a leader requires control without having to be in so many places at once, empowerment is the key. It is perhaps one of the few initiatives that reaps benefits for the individual first while enhancing the organisation. This is because:

- the workforce will discover ways to enhance efficiency and quality through the natural course of their work;

- everyone is clear about the individual and team direction they are heading in so there is less duplication of effort and conflict of purpose;

- staff are enabled before being empowered so fewer mistakes are likely;

- wastage of resources is easily identified and eliminated;

- employees share more in the 'mission' and are therefore prepared to give that little extra to achieve it (more for less is attained);

- money that might otherwise have been spent on incentive schemes can be invested in training/enabling with longer-term gains for the organisation.

It is understandable if you can't see what good driving looks like without at first recognising dangerous or inconsiderate driving. If the same is likely here, ask yourself whether any of the following symptoms are evident in your team or organisation at present:

- Staff are unproductive most of the time.
- Individuals seem to await further instructions from you before taking action, causing delays and deadlines to be missed.
- Everyone appears to be busy but not a lot seems to be achieved.
- Staff don't criticise the way things are done.
- Ideas or inputs from subordinates are not forthcoming.
- Staff are constantly being reprimanded for either acting without authority or for not showing initiative.
- Staff turnover is increasing.
- Customers are dissatisfied with particular aspects of service yet nothing has been done about it.
- Employees know what their jobs are, but they don't know what is expected of them.
- The finger of blame always has to point at someone.
- The left hand doesn't know what the right hand is doing.
- Management spends too much time doing other workers' tasks instead of managing.
- There is an acute absence of creativity and initiative.

If any of these symptoms are showing, ask yourself three questions:

1. Why is this happening?
2. How can I prevent it from happening again?
3. What will it look like when things are done well?

Establishing why it is happening will heighten your awareness – but don't guess, go and find out by talking to those involved (see the application of the Johari window below). Finding the answer to prevent it from happening again might put you in a better position to take control of the situation. However, stopping there may leave you applying 'reactive' solutions, causing you to be forever behind as you catch up with yesterday.

Organisations which ask 'what will it look like when things are done well?' are the ones which are proactive and better able to bring about the outcomes they seek. They spend time looking ahead and getting there rather than focusing on changing the past while losing touch with the future.

The empowerment window

Empowerment may not be rocket science, but I'm going to show you a model that has its basis in such an esteemed field. In 1973, Joseph Luft and Harry Ingham developed a model for 'soliciting feedback'. It may sound very mystical now but the Johari window was founded on the principles of telemetry that sent rockets to the Moon.

The essence of the model is to contrast the communications that exist between two parties in a relationship (be they work or social relationships) against where that relationship is heading. And its link with rocket science? Well, if you're sending a rocket to the Moon, at what point do you want to know if it's going to land on target? Is it sufficient to wait until five minutes before landing is scheduled to see where it is or might we need to know earlier?

The principle of telemetry is all about providing feedback as regularly as possible. The more frequent the feedback as to where the rocket is, the less any deviation from target is likely to be. And the less any deviation from target, the less effort required to get the rocket back on the correct course. Joe and Harry applied this to any relationship, reflecting in a matrix the extent to which we solicit feedback from the other party and how much we disclose about ourselves (see Figure 3.1).

There are questionnaires that can be used to elicit a person's 'window' for given relationships. These will reflect how open that relationship appears to be and whether a party has the right balance between asking questions (soliciting feedback) and telling or doing (self-disclosure). The vertical line can move along the top axis depending on how much feedback is sought. The horizontal line will move up or down the side axis to reflect the proportion of self-disclosure or openness.

The model is not designed to be an accurate scientific assessment and is primarily used as a self-perception tool. However, its real value is as a basis for discussion, particularly when the two parties compare both their

Figure 3.1 The Johari window

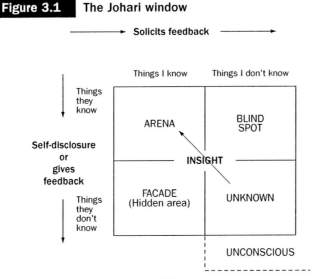

Source: Luft and Ingham, in Hanson (1973).

perceptions of the window. Each of the four segments (or panes) of the window has a significance: the top left is the one that should be the largest and most symmetrical if an open and effective relationship is to be achieved. Labelled as the 'Arena' in the Johari window, it is associated with the sports stadia and gladiator arenas where everyone within could see what was on show.

The same principle applies to the 'empowerment window' shown in Figure 3.2.

We can take the concept of the 'Arena' and refer to it as the 'Empowerment Zone'. This is where the skills and knowledge that the individual possesses are recognised by the leader. This may be because the leader has witnessed them in action, has assumed them within a qualification framework for which the individual has received accreditation, has assessed them through simulation, has received third-party appraisal or has even been told so by the individual.

The practical application of this window is in identifying within the zone all related skills and knowledge that could come into play in the scope of the individual's role. See what

Figure 3.2 The empowerment window

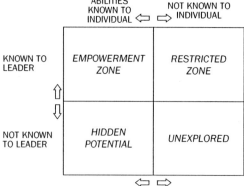

Adapted from Luft and Ingham, in Hanson (1973).

the individual is capable of and what tools you can equip them with, then scope the job. In contrast, by scoping the job first then identifying the individual to do it, we may end up with a nearest fit and the consequence of training needs to address or the individual feeling that they are being undervalued. The latter approach is fine so long as you have the training budget and resource, the time to wait, and the motivation skills to give the individual their sense of achievement and fulfilment.

The 'Restricted Zone' is worth knowing too. What does the individual not have the skills and knowledge to do? The same sources that were listed above would provide the answers here too. This box is the needs analysis box for the individual and until such needs have been addressed the individual should not be exposed to activities requiring them. Yet how often do I discover people who were tasked with making business presentations without first being given the knowledge of how to prepare and structure the content for their audience, and secondly not being enabled with techniques for delivery?

The application requires an empowerment window for each individual. 'Too much hassle' did I hear you say? Well you are not doing your job if you don't know the role you expect the individual to perform and the skills or knowledge they bring to it. You probably have this information available, but not in the visual framework of the window. An appraisal form may be the closest you get but that doesn't necessarily portray what the individual may be capable of – just how they've done so far. So opportunities may be missed.

Perhaps the best example I can relate of this concerns my younger brother, Nick. Many years ago he was working for a UK company that manufactured and installed wide-area networking (WAN) systems. His directors were about to welcome a very important visitor on a tour of the site but were struggling to find an interpreter who not only spoke fluent Russian but who knew the company's product and manufacturing process. As a European sales representative he had occasionally had a chat over a pie and a pint with the International Sales Director who had a vague recollection of Nick mentioning that he spoke Russian. Somehow, this was not recorded on an accessible database, but his abilities were proven in a rehearsal in which he showed the Russian Ambassador around the site. The company had almost overlooked his skills and knowledge profile – his Empowerment Zone – and for a while were not aware they had the solution to the problem in their own ranks. Not only did he know the company's product and manufacturing processes as a sales representative, but he also had a degree in Russian. He therefore accompanied Mr Gorbachev throughout his visit and was photographed alongside him on the front page of *Pravda*!

Until he put himself forward through a chance discussion, Nick's fluency in Russian was part of his 'Hidden Potential'. No one had asked him since his recruitment interview what skills or knowledge he had (whether perceived as immediately work-related or not!), and evidently it wasn't information that was accessible where it was needed. Perhaps the existence of an Empowerment Window would have changed that because it would have recorded fluency in Russian as one of his abilities, through initial discussions or reference to his qualifications at recruitment.

As Johari suggests, the more open the communication the more effective the relationship can prove to be. It provides a platform for exchanging information early in the leader–follower relationship, and then maintaining that flow. The information gathering doesn't have to be formal – a chat over a drink or meal can be quite revealing – but the knowledge gained should be recorded formally somewhere. So, as we saw in the first chapter, know what you know, get that hidden potential out in the open and enlarge that 'Empowerment Zone', balancing this with some enabling too.

The 'Unexplored' is where neither the individual nor the leader has information on aspects of the individual's skills or knowledge. While Nick's fluency in Russian may have been 'unexplored' by his directors, it clearly wasn't unexplored because Nick knew of his ability. It was in his 'known to him' column but also the 'not known to them' (the leader) row. Therefore, for the leader, it was Nick's hidden potential. Yet prior to studying Russian it would have been unexplored or untried. He – and they – would not know how capable or otherwise he was. Had he embarked on his degree course and failed then it would have found its way to the 'Restricted Zone'.

I'm also reminded here of a team exercise that I have used over a number of years, which appropriately enough is associated with the driving licence. It is based around the Highway Code in the UK and requires a team to arrive at an answer by group consensus to each question.

One such group had ignored the responses of an elderly team member because they assumed he must have passed his test so long ago that he would have to be guessing at the answers. Imagine their surprise when he obtained the highest individual score. Had they asked him the question they would have discovered that he had spent the previous four months reading through the Highway Code helping his daughter who was taking her driving test!

Similarly, one group knew that one of its members didn't in fact drive as he was picked up and taken into work by another member of the group – his boss! Yet again he was pretty much ignored though there was another factor at play; he was subordinate to the other group members and wasn't comfortable correcting them. When his score was found to be significantly higher than that of the others they asked him out of curiosity and politeness how that was possible. He reasoned that as drivers they perhaps had to react to signs or situations at a less conscious level, whereas as a passenger he had longer to see them and take them in and consider what they meant. Had they asked him the question earlier ...?

What is the moral of the story? Perhaps leaders (drivers) could do with consulting passengers more often and not make assumptions. The answers to questions can be extremely enlightening so it pays to ask the right ones at the right time.

It is quite common for participants on all levels of development programmes to bemoan the fact that their boss treats them as though they were untrustworthy, unreliable, incapable or just not interested. These same people often look outside work to get the responsibility and satisfaction that their employers don't provide for them. Perhaps you should discover what your followers achieve outside work and ask whether you are making the most of the resource you have. You may find there's a committee member, treasurer, sports team manager, fund-raiser, club captain or part-time skills coach that you're taking the wrong kind of advantage of.

So the empowerment window can help us to establish the extent to which we can stop interfering and let go, and the level of enabling that may be required.

The benefits

Perhaps to explore further the need for empowerment and the benefits that it brings we have to go back to our technology-driven industrial turmoil of the last century. The advent of new technology in coal mining, textile weaving and the automotive industry exposed a significant social consequence. This consequence was so great as to impact on any intended economic benefit, such that expected labour cost savings were countered by a reduction in productivity (whether through sickness, absenteeism or sabotage) and local communities dependent on these industries went into social and economic decline. The dilemma was that technological progress was fuelling social regression.

How then could industry strike the balance between technological gains and economic and social well-being?

As we referred to in Chapter 1, enter the Scandinavians. What Volvo and Saab achieved is now legend, but if we look at it more closely we see that it is also common sense. Give the workers a say in their own workplace and they'll be happier for it. The productivity gains and social lift surprised many observers. In the UK, for example, it seemed almost that the role of workers was to form themselves into trade unions to avoid doing what it was the bosses wanted. So to see the Scandinavians forming themselves into work groups to organise how they would best meet management's targets was wholly alien. Undoubtedly national culture played a part in breaking from traditional norms, and it is only with the passage of time and proven gains that the rest of the world has followed suit. At last someone had found the compromise to balance technological gains with economic and social well-being. It was a need fulfilled.

The benefits of this empowerment thus extend beyond the corporate model. Industry benefits from a more collaborative and less confrontational workforce. Productivity increases, and there is research to support that sickness, absenteeism and sabotage reduces. Social gains accrue through improved health, earnings being ploughed back into the local community through spending and the creation of an 'achieving' culture where the rewards for success are apparent. Throw in the trend for a work/life balance and we see that empowerment is both constructive and liberating.

A benefit sometimes overlooked but frequently pivotal to productivity gains through empowerment is its ability to capture the otherwise tacit knowledge of those nearest to the job in hand. Take, for example, the administrator who for years has had to follow prescribed guidelines to accomplish a task, always knowing that in fact there is a better way which equally achieves the firm's objectives or even improves upon them. Too often in a directive-driven organisation the better way of doing things is known and acknowledged among those performing a task but seldom gets aired up the chain of command or is otherwise ignored. Often it is the absence of incentives that keeps such initiatives under wraps. By enabling individuals to achieve outcomes for themselves, you incentivise them to find the better way, releasing a proprietary knowledge gained usually from years of experience. Such knowledge is tacit in that it is unlikely to have been written down in any of the firm's procedural guides and is instead embedded in the individuals closest to the task. Generally, a greater level of knowledge will generate a higher level of performance – hence, knowledge once more is providing the power.

Depending on your point of view, another benefit from empowerment is the creation of flatter hierarchies through self-regulating workgroups. Flatter hierarchies reduce the cost of having layers of unproductive supervisors and managers. It means that the workgroups take care of themselves, planning their own objectives and allocating related tasks. They work within the parameters set by a productive management, whose task is to set and implement the strategy through enabling the workforce.

Figure 3.3 indicates where the technical and operational knowledge exists within organisations. Yet the message it really conveys here is that those with authority to make change happen know least what needs to change. Unless the knowledge gap is bridged with open channels of communication, including feedback, many of the changes imposed will prove unproductive and more costly than anticipated.

Figure 3.3 Authority vs knowledge

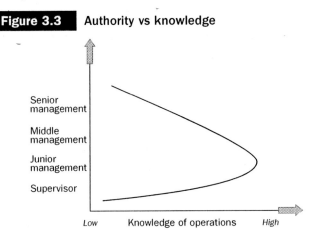

Where empowerment is needed most, it is also most likely that it will be harder to put in place. The organisations that would benefit are those where the emphasis is currently placed on subjective assessment of performance or where inputs are more important than outcomes. Contrast the following for a moment:

subjective vs objective
inputs vs outcomes
measurable vs important
quantity vs quality
personality vs performance

Where the organisation has systems and practices that draw our attention to aspects on the left-hand side, employees may experience high levels of dissatisfaction while the company itself misses out on its true growth potential.

Let's review what the implications are.

Subjective vs objective

As leaders we tend to have our own ideas on what should be achieved, and more often than not we have already worked out what is required to achieve it as well. So long as the 'criteria' by which achievement is measured stays in the leader's head, judgement will be subjective because the factors involved are known only to the subject (the leader) who carries out the assessment on the object (the activity).

On the other hand, were the criteria attributed to the activity made known and available to everyone carrying out that activity or passing judgement on its achievement, such judgement could be objective because the object that is being judged has the performance indicators already assigned to it. This will enable anyone making a judgement to arrive at the same conclusion.

Naturally, for the above to be true such objective criteria shouldn't leave room for subjective influence: words like effective or appropriate are open to different interpretations by the subject carrying out assessment on the object. Instead, describe what effective and appropriate actually look like.

Further room is left for subjectivity when insufficient criteria are attributed to the activity. So if someone thought they had done a great job, having met all the criteria for sailing a boat from one port to another, only for the leader to introduce another criteria at the end which was not achieved, then the sailor had not been truly empowered. Frustration would set in alongside a lack of trust in the leader.

Inputs vs outcomes

> Give a man a fish and you feed him for a day: teach a
> man to fish and you feed him for life.

In the adage above, which half represents an input and
which an outcome? I even write this with bated breath as it
is not a contrast that is easy to catch.

I see feeding the fish to the man is like giving him the input
and outcome simultaneously. His focus and expectation is
that someone else will have worked out how to obtain the
fish; he is just left to attain the end result of eating it. In fact,
his only ability could be to eat fish.

Yet teaching the man to fish puts the focus of attention on
the man's ability to be self-sufficient with regard to eating
fish. He is being enabled to achieve a specific output or
outcome that he then becomes dependent on.

If he is only taught one technique and shown one place to
fish then he may feed himself for life if things remain
constant. But what if that particular fish was in very short
supply, or fish had become wise to the technique and evaded
capture? Nothing in life is ever constant and being prepared
for change is half the battle.

If we restrict ourselves with such blinkered focus on the
inputs it would be all too easy to be caught hook, line and
sinker when we are unable to adapt to achieve desired
outcomes. The end result (outcomes) should always be more
important than the means to the end (inputs).

Measurable vs important (quantity vs quality)

What gets measured gets done! How true that invariably is.
So how much easier is it to measure quantity rather than
quality?

Most leaders are guilty of measuring what they can measure, then making this important. Hence we can measure the volume of calls made or received, the units shipped or bought, the number of staff present and the amount of money coming in or going out.

However, in giving too much focus to the measurables we may be in danger of losing sight of other things which are more important but harder to measure.

At a call centre in the Middle East not so long ago, I witnessed an occasion when the LCD display for one section indicated that 43 per cent of calls were being abandoned when the acceptable level was no more than 6 per cent. I overheard the call centre manager berate the team supervisor who tried to defend his team by rationalising that he had two agents off sick while the advert for a new promotion had gone out a week early. Such a volume of calls was not anticipated for that day.

So what did the manager suggest – or should I say, dictate? He wanted all waiting calls diverted to their Administration Department, whose remit had nothing to do with calls of that nature. Within twenty minutes the calls abandoned ratio was down to the acceptable level and the manager was pleased, but what of the customers and Admin? Customers were being told by Admin that they had come through to the wrong department and would have to call back later as lines were busy. Admin couldn't get on with their job and customers were infuriated that they'd been treated so off-handedly, many of them increasing call volumes further when they attempted to complain.

It all represented a classic example of making the measurable important rather than looking for ways of making what is important measurable. The introduction in the UK of National Occupational Standards for call centre operations has since gone some way to providing a description of what it should look like when the quality is in place, rather than merely the quantity.

Personality vs performance

Something fundamental to attaining empowerment and good performance is frequent feedback. As we have seen earlier, empowerment does not mean abdication of a leader's involvement and responsibility. It merely alters the focus of it.

Performance appraisal should be carried out at least annually, but it should only then be a summary of the 'dripping tap' approach. Don't just turn the water full on and then off at appraisal time but give feedback, a little and often, in small drips through the intervening period.

Yet remember it is an appraisal of 'performance' and not 'personality'. If outcomes (standards) have been used descriptively to determine what good performance looks like, sounds like and feels like, then feedback should also be descriptive of what you saw, heard or felt in relation to the performance criteria stated. This will help to depersonalise the feedback and prevent it being focused on the personality. The attainment of performance improvement and not personality assassination is the desired outcome.

Without objective performance standards and outcomes, such performance appraisal is so much harder to achieve. But the real beauty of having them in place at the outset is that the appraisee can self-assess. You'll know empowerment is being achieved when they are more critical of their performance than you would have been and they have already identified development needs for you to discuss with them.

Up until now it might appear that empowerment is only to be found at the outset of tasks or activities being assigned.

It is often overlooked that it needs to be used throughout the cycle of people management.

It would be wrong to think that once people are empowered they don't make any mistakes at all or that performances are always at their optimum. However, seeking an improvement from them becomes so much easier. The following process is advised for 'improving performance in others', and usually the sticking point is that there was no agreement that a performance standard existed other than in the mind of the assessor. The employee does what they are told to do and waits to find out if it is good enough.

However, if the guidelines in this book are followed in agreeing outcomes at the outset, then it becomes so much easier to monitor and manage the performance of teams and individuals.

By applying the process shown in Figure 3.4 the individual is being empowered to provide the solution with the knowledge they have. If the outcomes have not been expressed let alone agreed with them in the first instance, they would not have the knowledge to provide the solution and commit to it.

The sound of empowerment

Another indicator of a need to switch to a more empowering style of leadership is when you hear managers say:

'I want to know exactly what's happening'

'That's not how I would do it. I'd ...'

'We'll do what I suggest unless anyone has any problems with that'

Figure 3.4 Improving performance in others

1. **Describe, in a friendly manner, the situation to be improved**
   - Focus on the situation, not the other person
   - Refer to the current standard and agreed outcomes
   - Seek their acknowledgement that the situation exists

2. **Ask for the other person's help in resolving the situation**
   - Refer to their previous good performances
   - Use 'we'

3. **Discuss the causes of the current situation**
   - Use open-ended questions
   - Avoid 'blame'

4. **Identify and record possible solutions**
   - Encourage them to suggest solutions
   - Use the standard as the reference point
   - Reaffirm agreement on the outcomes if necessary

5. **Decide on specific action to be taken by each of you**
   - Allow them to feel that they have contributed to the solution rather than had it imposed on them
   - Ensure that the action is achievable and measurable

6. **Agree on the timing and nature of a follow-up**
   - Set dates
   - Provide a written record of agreed action for reference at the follow-up

'How the hell did this happen?'

'I'll tell you what they'll think, they'll think ...'

'Must I end up doing everything myself?'

'You had no right to do that ...'

'Don't do anything without consulting me'

The more people hear these utterances, the more they will be left thinking:

'It's about time management did something'

'There's no point, s/he won't listen'

'How do you want us to do it this time?'

'I need to speak to my manager'

'I'm not paid to take the blame, so I won't bother'

'What do I do next? I'd better wait'

So what does empowerment sound like? For the empowering leader it will sound very much like:

'My door is open if you need me'

'Will that approach meet our criteria?'

'Let's discuss your ideas'

'How can we solve this problem?'

'Ask the customers for their input'

'When could you get this done by?'

'Thank you. Well done'

As for those being empowered, they will be thinking: 'I've got an idea' and 'how could I best achieve that?' They will be saying: 'What will it look like when it's done well?' and 'Yes! I can get that sorted for you'. They will feel valued and derive satisfaction from the job itself.

And how will it look? You will see people giving more, working more purposefully with others, producing results, using their initiative and displaying a 'can do' attitude rather than 'what can I get away with?'

Motivation theory

We all think we know what motivating others requires, yet do we always make that distinction between motivating and, simply, not demotivating? It's the difference between offering the carrot and merely taking away those awful greens!

Money is a significant factor employed in motivating people. It allows us the means to satisfy our material needs but it can also be seen as a measure of recognition and success. In many situations money does get people to work but it does not necessarily get people to work harder. The calculative use of money as a motivator can create expectations among staff that will create difficulties in the long term. Instead, we can learn from the research of two eminent names in motivation theory: Abraham Maslow and Frederick Herzberg.

Maslow

In 1949 Maslow classified people's needs in the form of a hierarchy. This identifies five distinct levels of needs with the most basic needs at the bottom (see Figure 3.5).

Maslow suggests that a need will only become a motivator if it is not currently satisfied; furthermore, it would not be possible to address needs at a higher level in the hierarchy until those below have been met. Consequently, needs are

Figure 3.5 — Maslow's hierarchy and Herzberg's findings

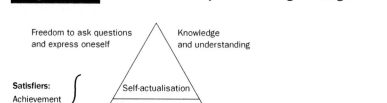

never static; they change over time and are conditioned by events around us. For example, if you are starving you want to be given food or the means to buy it, not praise and extra responsibility. Likewise, if you are warm enough, more heat being provided will not motivate you.

Descriptions of Maslow's 'innate needs of man' are given below.

- The *Basic* need level is for survival today – the need for food, water and shelter. Nowadays this would be reflected in the wages to cover provision of these essential items or the provision of these items themselves.

- *Security* is the need to know that you can have the basic needs met tomorrow and the day after. So wages today are helpful, but the security of wages next week or next month are paramount. Can the mortgage be sustained?

- *Belonging* is the need to be identified with a group of people or an organisation where there is the opportunity for social interaction. I can sustain my basic survival so now I want to relate to the people I am surviving with!

Being labelled as part of a team or wearing a uniform can often satisfy this level, so long as its focus is positive.

- *Ego-status* is the next logical development where, having been accepted by a group you want an individual identity and recognition within it. Perhaps being acknowledged as the spokesperson, specialist, agony aunt or team leader may provide the motivation. It is where self-esteem and feeling valued feature strongly.

- *Self-actualisation*, at the pinnacle of the pyramid, is where you no longer meet the challenges set by others as a means to an end, but you meet your own personal challenges and aims. This would assume the other needs are all satisfied, and is the reason why people give up well-paid but possibly stressful jobs to do something 'they've always wanted to do' – like climb the Himalayas! Responsibility and achievement, as well as challenge, are eagerly sought.

So from Basic to midway through Belonging, people will do almost any work: from there to the pinnacle the work itself matters.

However, Maslow also identified two other needs that are often overlooked because they are not within the hierarchy. They are not applied at any one level because he saw them as being ever-present; they sit outside the pyramid.

- The need for *Freedom to ask questions and express oneself* supports the concept and acceptance that we are all individuals, with individual concerns, interests, ideas and opinions. And we like our existence to be acknowledged.

- Meanwhile our need for *Knowledge and understanding* is what distinguishes us from the animal kingdom and nurtures our development.

These last two underpin the principles of empowerment, while gaining further support from the recognition that receiving respect and trust, and feeling valued, motivates.

Herzberg

Herzberg later analysed factors quoted by employees as being causes of satisfaction and dissatisfaction at work. What he noticed was that the factors associated with one were quite different from those associated with the other. Hence, removing the dissatisfaction factors did not necessarily lead to motivation, while increasing the levels of satisfaction did not necessarily reduce dissatisfaction.

- *Satisfiers* (motivation factors)
  - Achievement
  - Responsibility
  - Recognition
  - Work itself
  - Advancement
- *Dissatisfiers* (hygiene factors)
  - Company policy
  - Working conditions
  - Salary
  - Supervision
  - Interpersonal relations

The dissatisfiers were equivalent to the lower level needs identified by Maslow, and Herzberg called them the 'hygiene factors': as with washing your hands, there comes a point when your hands won't get any cleaner no matter how much soap you apply! The satisfiers were labelled 'motivation factors' and supported Maslow's earlier findings that came from Belonging, Ego-status and Self-actualisation.

As leaders you have a key role to play in motivating your subordinates. You have a responsibility to ensure that you get the most out of your staff, but remember that it may not be possible with only one well-worn carrot!

So when we add the satisfiers to Maslow's theory, there is even more support for empowerment as it also motivates through levels of involvement in the work itself.

4

Enabling individuals and teams

Letting go

Consider for a moment your own position as a leader. On the continuum shown in Figure 4.1, where would you place yourself on the management scale?

Jobs are generally comprised of any combination of three skill sets:

- technical skills – and knowledge – that enable you to carry out procedural or dexterous tasks to produce an end product or service;
- interpersonal skills that enable you to liaise with customers, suppliers, colleagues and just about anyone else (no job can exist in total isolation); and
- conceptual skills that enable ideas and plans to be conceived and formulated.

The continuum identifies the extent to which these skill sets are likely to be required as you progress up the management hierarchy.

If you see yourself on the lower rung of the management hierarchy, at supervisor level, then you would be expected to be a technical practitioner still within your particular field of work. Your technical skills and knowledge are still very much called upon, and you are likely to be performing that

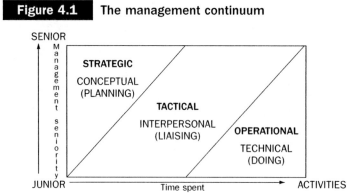

Figure 4.1   The management continuum

technical role still while also overseeing the work of others doing the same activity. The likelihood is that you arrived at the supervisor level, or emerged as a leader, through your proficiency as a technician. Those technical skills need not be complex but merely reflect the inputs necessary to perform at an operational level.

When you progress from being a supervisor to becoming a first-line manager or middle manager, the continuum indicates that the need to plan becomes a part of the role. Significantly, however, it also indicates that this is possible because some of the technical skills are no longer employed. In other words, there is something you have to let go of to make room for the planning to come in.

This, perhaps more than most factors, can impinge on first-line and middle management's ability to empower. If you have risen through the ranks but have not yet been properly enabled with the new skills set, the chances are you will fall into the comfort zone of what you know you know. You will be reluctant to let go of a skills set that gave you success and you will be drawn to taking part in a role that is no longer yours. However good your intentions, this regression will be perceived by those still in the role as interference. Either you will be rolling up your sleeves and 'mucking in' or you will be telling others how to do their job.

Though technical skills make way for conceptual ones, it is important to note that the need for interpersonal skills remains constant as you progress through the levels. We cannot avoid interacting with other people though the nature and outcomes of the interactions will differ from supervisor to chief executive. This is where a new 'picture' has to be painted for the change in roles. The new manager needs to be shown how to let go: this is not the enabling they are given, however, as the focus is on adding new skills rather than releasing some.

Without letting go, something will suffer. Usually, this is a significant reason why promoted managers find themselves working longer hours than before. 'Presenteeism' may have a part to play, but it helps to interfere in your old job so there is the excuse to be present as much as possible.

The continuum also indicates that the most senior executives spend their time conceiving strategies and plans, though it would be unfair to suggest that they do very little.

Letting the individual have a say in his or her own destination is what matters here. There are a number of tools for doing this, as we'll see later. Perhaps communication up the line is not what you would like it to be, or staff turnover is high and even morale has not turned up for work. Inefficiencies and lack of effectiveness can all point to the need for redrafting the scope of the licence, clarifying the vision(s) with individuals and equipping them with the right skills, knowledge and tools for their own jobs.

Those who pass the driving test at the first attempt either have great natural ability or they know clearly what is required to pass and they work at it. Yet, as the leading empowerment model suggests, there will be some who may need more lessons and more tests and who are not yet ready to be empowered for certain activities. Just be sure that if they're expected to take the test in a Ferrari the lessons aren't taken in a Ford Escort.

Training and development

Perhaps the biggest failing in enabling individuals and teams is that leaders look too often for a best-fit, pre-existing training solution. Such a solution may not have been designed to achieve the specifics you are after. Perhaps it's a sales training programme that uses examples of selling insurance to the end-user, such as income protection to the employer and motor insurance to the motorist. If, however, the individual or team has to sell it to brokers, perhaps the course won't equip them with the appropriate skills and knowledge of why a broker will buy into their product rather than the end-user. Sometimes it's a presentation skills course that offers all sorts of tips on delivery yet fails to enable the individual to plan and structure the appropriate content and visuals for the audience. As the former is usually more symptomatic of the latter, time will have been wasted merely looking at delivery.

There is already an excellent book that addresses getting value for money from training. I wrote it in 1991 and the principles have not changed, though the National Occupational Standards have at last proven to be as significant a guide as I suggested they might. *How to Take a Training Audit*, published by Kogan Page, is a reference text at many colleges and train-the-trainer institutions yet the chapters on 'Auditing the identification of training needs' and 'Auditing the training solution' should really be read by leaders and feature in management development programmes. However, I shall provide a snapshot here of the key issues.

1. Start with desired outcomes, not desired inputs.

2. Consider all aspects of an activity that you measure against but don't always express.

3. Use an appropriate method of assessment to identify training (learning) or enabling needs.

4. Express the need specifically, not with the solution already determined.

5. Tailor the solution to the individual, not the other way around.

1. Start with desired outcomes, not desired inputs

When designing training (or learning) solutions it is preferable to determine firstly what the quality of the end product should be. What should the learner be capable of achieving? What will it look like when they are competent? By doing this we can focus more on the options available to achieve the outcomes.

If we started instead with the inputs – the things we wanted to impart – we are in danger of limiting someone's ability to only one route or method. Outcomes tend to remain the same for any given job, yet the methodology changes frequently nowadays. It's hard to adapt to change though when all that you've known is a fixed route.

2. Consider all aspects of an activity that you measure against but don't always express

When completing tasks there are usually explicit requirements we have to meet. These are typically a deadline and some quantitative value that is measurable. The qualitative aspect is often left to the subjective judgement of the person requiring the task to be done. Next time, make notes on what you looked for, critiqued or were particularly impressed with – thereafter express these 'qualitative needs' too, up front.

3. Use an appropriate method of assessment to identify training (learning) or enabling needs

For example, how would you identify the training needs for each of the following:

- a salesperson who consistently fails to convert visits to sales?

- a manager whose staff are regularly absent without adequate cover provided?

- a machine operative who produces defects above the tolerance level?

- a trainer who frequently receives below average assessment on course feedback?

- an organisation which is about to change over to a networked computer-based system from its traditional paper-based approach?

- a salesperson who sees far fewer potential customers per week than her colleagues?

- a fork-lift truck driver who seems to have an accident at least once a month?

- a receptionist who is new to the company and the job?

- an order clerk who registers considerably less incoming calls per hour than his colleagues?
- an organisation that is about to introduce a standards-based performance review system where no reviews have previously taken place?

For each of the circumstances above there may well be a number of different factors that give rise to an inadequate performance, and they may not be the fault of the individual, or may not be as a consequence of something obvious. In the first situation, the assumption would be to send the salesperson on a 'closing the sale' programme. What if the cause, however, had more to do with poor qualifying of prospects and his appointments were all with the wrong people? How do you know that, in the third example, the machine itself isn't at fault?

Observation is by far the best method to establish needs, in as real an environment as possible. Underpinning knowledge can be sought through a question and answer session but there are people who talk a good job but can't put it into practice. Leaders require good vision – this should also include their observation skills.

4. Express the need specifically, not with the solution already determined

Once the cause of the unsatisfactory performance has been established, the cause should then be expressed and not the solution. An example of the correct approach, as opposed to the incorrect one, was provided with regard to sales training at the start of this section on training and development (see p. 57).

5. Tailor the solution to the individual, not the other way around

An effective training solution addresses the needs of the trainee rather than just those of the subject itself. Just because a course provided the solution for one person, it may not be right for another, unless the course itself is flexible and trainee-focused rather than subject-focused.

Gaining commitment

Another 'model' that has some relevance here is the 'Leadership Grid' devised by Blake and Mouton (see Figure 4.2). This grid developed Blanchard and Hersey's thinking into an organisational context, contrasting 'concern for people' with 'concern for production' (task achievement).

Figure 4.2 **Blake and Mouton's leadership grid**

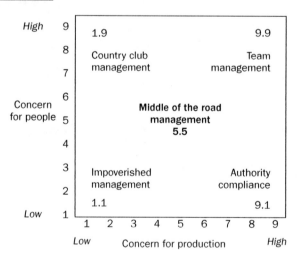

Where is empowerment? In the model in Figure 4.2 it would fall along a corridor from 'Middle of the road' to 'Team management'. Why? This is because empowerment matches the concern for production with the concern that the people know what is required of them, and that they have the right tools, skills and knowledge to achieve it. Empowerment is very much a team tool. Initially, work can be accomplished while maintaining workforce morale. Meanwhile, the trust and respect that gets built up through true empowerment leads ultimately to a workforce that is more committed and involved.

During a workshop to establish what empowerment looked like, sounded like and felt like within a major consulting firm, there were two characteristics that consistently appeared at the top:

1. Clarifies objectives

2. Respects and trusts others.

It was interesting that while the firm expressed the empowerment of its staff as one of its values, the staff did not feel that it practised what it preached. The above characteristics were drawn to the top by their absence. What also became clear in the ensuing discussions was that objectives usually arrived as tasks with appended deadlines. They were not SMART (Specific, Measurable, Achievable, Rewarding and Time-bound) and staff had not been empowered to question them. What they wanted to know by 'clarifying the objectives' was what did the completed activity look like when the boss was happy with it?

When asked why 'provides the vision' appeared much lower down their list, the response was that the organisation was frequently espousing where it saw itself and what it wanted to be, and it even provided statistics to keep staff informed. However, it wasn't a vision in which they could readily identify themselves. The bigger picture was there, but the smaller picture that the individual created or starred in was often missing.

By contrast, the same exercise conducted with over 300 managers from a facilities management organisation placed 'provides the vision' near the top of desirable characteristics, along with 'respects and trusts others' and 'clarifies objectives'. In the early days this was because it was also absent. Many of the managers had been with the organisation when it was a public sector enterprise. Privatisation and the accrual of many fragmented projects all over the UK meant that very few employees had any sense of identity with the new company and only knew their own areas of responsibility. They were so in the dark as to what they belonged to that anything shoved in their direction would have been welcome.

Fortunately our programme allowed for such feedback to the directors and gave them a role to play. Gradually, the new vision was described to the masses and new innovations were introduced to defragment communication within the group. In the latter stages of the programme 'provides the vision' was placed at the top on merit, owing to the impact that it had on helping individuals to identify themselves in the big picture. They could see the direction and rationale of where they were going and could progress unhindered by uncertainty and the fear of letting go of yesterday.

The same exercise can be used in your team, area of responsibility or organisation to establish the characteristics that matter to the followers. They may well come up with some of their own, but involving them in the discussion is a valuable starting point on the road to instigating an empowerment culture. (See Appendix 1 for the exercise brief.)

For empowerment to be more than just a leadership style and become the culture of an organisation, it must be applied consistently. The exercise was used across the spectrum of management levels, including the directors, so that perceptions could be contrasted. In asking the directors to rank the same characteristics, they placed 'sees the customer as most important' at the top of the list. Everyone else, almost without exception, placed that characteristic at the bottom, suggesting it was least important from the list. It had, though, already been acknowledged that all the characteristics were important – we were merely establishing their relative priority from each group's perspective.

Other groups felt that the directors placed too much emphasis on aspects external to the organisation, and if more attention were given to the internal issues then everything would fall into place to provide excellent customer service. Staff saw themselves as more important, particularly in their context as the means to the end. Management saw the provision of customer service as the end result, whereas the directors betrayed the fact that they saw that as merely the means to their end. They saw money and increasing the dividend for shareholders as the end result, with customers as merely the means. This was hardly surprising at the time because they were appointed by venture capitalists and were themselves significant shareholders.

It's fair to say that the outcomes sought by the directors were different to those sought at operational level, but were nonetheless valid for the mission to which they were assigned. But therein lies the gift of true leaders. True leaders see not just their own desired outcomes but those that exist en route to the ultimate destination. They see the outcomes that others achieve and which are likely to be expressed without recourse to the words 'dividend' and 'shareholder value'. True leaders sell the same destination in different words for all to identify with. They don't just see it from their own standpoint – they stand where everyone else is so they can see how things look from there too.

So leaders need vision, but not one that's wearing blinkers. And the only way they can get the full picture is to exchange perspectives on a regular basis from elsewhere in the team.

Remember:

- Empathise
- Manage expectations
- Provide vision and involvement
- Open communication channels
- Want to let go
- Enable individuals and the team
- Respect and trust their abilities

Core content

Some of the essentials which individuals should have to demonstrate before being empowered are:

- the ability to ask open questions to gather all relevant facts (see Figure 4.3);
- listening skills which reflect a high retention of input;
- the confidence to clarify their own understanding and the understanding of others;
- clarity and conciseness of written and oral communication to avoid misunderstandings;

Figure 4.3 The enabling cocktail

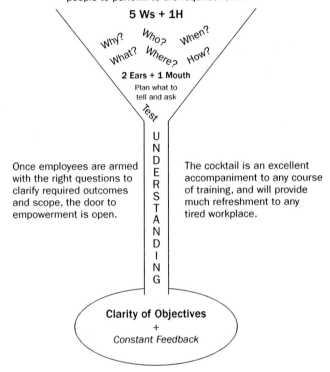

This cocktail reflects the importance of communication in helpng people to perform to the required level.

5 Ws + 1H

Why? Who? When?
What? Where? How?

2 Ears + 1 Mouth

Plan what to tell and ask

Test

UNDERSTANDING

Once employees are armed with the right questions to clarify required outcomes and scope, the door to empowerment is open.

The cocktail is an excellent accompaniment to any course of training, and will provide much refreshment to any tired workplace.

Clarity of Objectives
+
Constant Feedback

- management of their time so that priorities are properly addressed and agreed deadlines are met;

- the ability to structure a case for influencing others to take a particular course of action.

Empowerment is 99.9 per cent communication, so the above should be the foundation on which to build.

Perhaps it should be noted that the cocktail is in a Martini glass – a tool that can therefore be used any time, any place and anywhere!

In the next chapter we will see how important selling, rather than telling, really is.

5

Implementing empowerment in the organisation

Providing the framework

In all the environments where my colleagues and I assisted in establishing an empowerment culture, we have always taken a 'snapshot' of what the culture currently looks like and sounds like. People so readily identify with non-empowerment that the impending change in culture gains their support from day one. It also produces some scepticism that 'they' (management) will never change.

Having trained as a general human resources (HR) practitioner, with a specialism in training, I find that the root of all trouble – and, therefore, the source of the solution too – can lie in the systems and procedures that managers are faced with before they even join a company: job descriptions which were invariably meaningless with lists of activities and not much focus on accomplishments, recruitment based upon a vague vision of what the role encompasses and more hope than assurance that the candidate selected has the potential to do the job.

So how can the systems help? Well, I see empowerment as an equation where:

What the outcomes look like + Enabling
= The licence to get on with the job

There are already HR tools that are available to support this, such as the National Occupational Standards referred to in Chapter 1. So the equation becomes:

Competences + Competencies
= A framework that supports training,
job evaluation and career development

Here 'Competences' can represent the job description (the outcomes of the job) while 'competencies' reflect what HR practitioners would know as the person specification. These two fundamental documents can actually be drawn together into what I have called 'the job profile'.

The example shown in Appendix 2 is a job profile developed for a facilities management company. At the time of compiling the job profile there were some issues emerging with three managers who had similar jobs but quite different employment and qualification backgrounds. A number of management development modules had been put together based around the needs of the team as expressed by the general operations manager.

The opportunity was also taken to interview each jobholder and establish their own perceptions of the job they had been doing for between six months and a year. Gradually, through these discussions and those on the modules, it became apparent that one or two were spending too long in the office and were not getting out to the locations and meeting with the NHS Trust customer on the site(s) for which they were responsible. When I suggested we sought clarification from the job descriptions, there were more questions raised than answers given.

As was fairly typical of most job descriptions they were quite general in describing the activities undertaken and pointed more to inputs than outcomes. What was not clear was what the job itself looked like when it was being done to the desired standard. The general operations manager had one idea, the jobholders three others, and the 'customers' yet more.

Duties and responsibilities on the original job description included:

- Manage and lead delivery of catering, portering and domestic services through effective operational procedures as required by contract documentation.

- Develop an effective facilities management strategy to deliver value-for-money services, which contributes to business objectives within the parameters of the client brief.

- Provide leadership and professional support to operational managers ensuring that personal development needs in line with business objectives are identified and met.

- Establish and maintain a positive working relationship with Trust client managers.

Having seen the above, it was hoped that the contract documentation would provide more of an objective measure or outcome – but it didn't. The terminology used was vague and subjective and stipulated activities without a qualitative standard.

The client brief and business objectives offered some indicators of performance but the decisions on whether a desired standard had been met seemed to rest finally with the Trust client managers. They determined whether or not they were happy, because there was room for them to do so. Even the jobholders had a different idea of what 'a positive working relationship' meant – despite some client feedback.

The confusions in interpretation were beginning to manifest themselves in conflicts internally and with the client. No amount of management development training was going to resolve this without going back to basics. It was time to ask: 'What does "effective" look like?' 'How do you know when you've provided leadership and professional support?' 'How big a contribution has to be made to the business objectives?'

Starting with the original job descriptions it was possible to pick out duties or responsibilities that fell under the broader headings of planning and organising, leadership, customer interfacing, reporting, and training and development. This gave a breakdown of where many of the tasks and key achievements of the role sat. Despite being prepared to alter these as the full extent and measures of the job were unearthed, all outcomes fell comfortably into these categories.

Activities were observed, discussions were held with all parties, including the client, and questions were constantly asked until an objective measure could be expressed that pointed to evidence of it being done to the necessary standard.

That word 'evidence' is crucial. It points to where the end result is found and without it the activity cannot be monitored properly. The 'Sources of evidence' column (see Appendix 2) indicates to the jobholder where their success will be measured, while to the leader it is also a ready map of where to go to assess performance if observation is not always possible.

The third column is where the job meets the jobholder. It is possible for each activity or outcome to identify the skills or knowledge required to achieve it. Broad labels may be acceptable here because the specific is suggested in the 'outcomes' column anyway. This amounts then to the list of 'competencies' that are required to do the job well. You can go further and indicate the skills and knowledge that the jobholder must bring with them, or those that you can provide them with once they arrive.

In short, the job profile can be used at the recruitment stage to identify the person specification and ensure you bring in the right people to the role in the first place. It also presents a clear picture of the role to any incumbent, so they know what they are in for. It can be used by the jobholder as a guide to what must be done on a daily or weekly basis, and it can be used by their manager or leader to monitor performance and contribute to identifying development needs. It becomes a working document rather than one that is ignored once the jobholder starts.

When the job profile was complete, it highlighted that two of the current jobholders were not experienced enough or qualified to do the job. The lack of detail on the original job description led to a lack of detailed questioning at interview. There was insufficient knowledge of legislation that had an impact on the role and, in one case, no experience of running a catering operation. Hence a new role emerged for the catering manager who had previously had a difficult relationship with his less experienced but authoritative boss.

I still find it amusing when I read, at the bottom of job descriptions, words to the effect of 'the contents of this job description are not exhaustive and may be amended in the light of changing business and client needs'. It really means, 'the job description is not helpful and we can ask you to do anything else we want anyway'.

It's no wonder that we can't have an empowerment culture when, as an organisation, we don't know what we really want jobholders to achieve. Yet there should be no need for the 'proviso' statement if employees are involved and consulted should the business and client needs ever change.

Consider the alternatives:

No competences + No competencies
= A lack of direction, variations in quality
and an ineffective or inefficient workforce

Competencies – Competences
= A subjective personality assessment that
focuses on inputs rather than outcomes

Competences – Competencies
= An objective and evidential benchmark of
performance though lacking the necessary
skills/knowledge profile to carry out the role

To see ourselves as others see us is a gift, so we're told. Maybe to get others to see what we see is as big a gift, and those mechanisms at the core of empowerment will achieve just that.

Assessing ability

Referring to our driving licence analogy again, how comfortable might the leader be letting someone else drive his or her brand new car? It's his or her car but control is given to someone else.

Assuming they're sharing the same journey, to what extent will the leader take the back seat and enjoy having the time to relax or concentrate on something else? Or will they sit in the front and provide instructions?

Of course there are a number of factors that would determine your answer:

- the known experience or ability of the driver;
- the status and value of the car;

- the leader's desire for control and

- whether the driver was informed in the first place about the destination, timeframe and scope of the journey.

The concept of the test itself raises issues in favour of the culture of empowerment and the expression of performance standards. Take the contrast between a traditional approach to assessment and the application of outcomes, otherwise known in the UK as competences, shown in Figure 5.1.

We have grown up in a culture that accredits people for what they can remember, and one that allows for degrees of failure. There are millions walking around today who trust the knowledge they recorded during an exam, because they passed it. As no one told them the 30–40 per cent they got wrong, how do they know that they know what they know?!

Figure 5.1   Traditional vs competence-based assessment

Traditional	Competence-based
One set day of the year	Evidence gathered over a period of time
Examined on only a part of a syllabus	Evidence against all standards
May choose from exam questions in some cases	All competences must be met
Measures retention of input	Assessment is focused on outcomes
Results are graded and influenced by the performance of others doing the same exam	No comparisons with others and no grading – either a candidate is competent or not yet competent
The pass mark can allow for 50% to be wrong!	Any errors highlight development needs that are addressed before reassessment
No feedback is given on which answers were wrong!!	The framework relies on feedback and uses it constructively

I was part of a team that helped to identify and introduce competences (National Standards) for operational firefighters within the Fire and Rescue Services in the UK. If I were a firefighter – and my life was reliant on my knowledge and that of my colleagues – I would want to be sure that I knew what I knew: just as importantly I'd want that extra reassurance that my colleagues know they know what they know. Yet how many could safely and effectively apply bolt-cutters or use breathing apparatus appropriately if it has been over three years since they last had to do it? How many could effectively apply a guideline through a smoking building to find their way to safety rather than get tangled and confused with another team's guideline and take the wrong turn?

Now they must revisit and renew their competence on a regular basis through drills and simulations and it is up to the 'leaders' of the crew, watch or station to ensure that everyone knows they know what being safe and effective looks like. This is made easier for them by the National Occupational Standards (NOS) for the Fire Services that clarify what each role looks like when it's meeting expectations of performance.

In the example above, the need to have a shared and unambiguous vision may have been motivated by matters of life and death. It may even have been prompted by a desire for cost-effectiveness. What is clear now though is that steps have been taken which focus on the individual, and they now have the vision that empowers them to assess and address their own needs in safer environments.

The equivalent in the commercial sector could still come down to a matter of survival, if not actually life and death. Having the opportunity to learn the skills and acquire the knowledge in 'safer environments' may still apply, rather than risk exposure of costly errors to customers.

So modifying your 'systems' for recruitment, ongoing appraisal, staff development and communication will all greatly assist in bedding in an empowerment culture.

Use 'job profiling' or at least review your appraisal forms so that they refer to outcomes and measurable achievement, not subjective evaluation. I remember one internationally renowned organisation that had the same appraisal system for managers as for the production line. When I asked how they could assess an operator on a machine for 'tenacity', particularly on a scale of poor, average and exceptional, they realised the futility of learning appraisal interviewing skills when the tool they had to use was inappropriate. Management was soon empowered as a by-product of the training to design a system that worked across the organisation, even though it meant a different form for the machine operators and production hands.

The same outcome was necessary at a major international consultancy. They preached empowerment but it became evident that their 'performance evaluation' system didn't have much room for objective setting and clarification of outcomes and it left too much room for subjectivity. 'Evidence' soon became a word that was used in support of staff rather than against them! The presumption that appraisees were already enabled was also corrected.

Communication is 99 per cent of the answer to most of the problems in the work environment. Let's look, for example, at how empowerment can be applied within the three levels of leadership identified as episodic, ambient and organisational.

Episodic leadership

Episodic is the leadership provided by junior (first-line) managers and supervisors, and it addresses the task, team and individual needs. It is therefore important that the episodic leader describes the desired outcomes of tasks and activities and enables the individual or team by providing the tools to do the job and access to resources and the skills and knowledge, if they are not already there.

For each task or activity there may be a number of different outcomes that describe how well it has to be done. As an example, if we explore the activity of redecorating a room, we may not be complete if we merely set the objective that the room looks freshly painted in the chosen colour. It may be stating what it looks like, but to establish what it will look like when it is done well will be enhanced by the application of TED:

Tell me why you want it redecorated.
Explain what constraints have to be imposed.
Describe what you will be looking for at the end.

The end of the activity is when we cast the critical eye over the work and start to make more explicit those things that really matter. They had probably always mattered but had remained unconscious or unspoken until they became visible.

Yet when the question is in the guise of a more specific instruction, it is amazing how much more you can unearth. Using the selection from TED to precede the question is a powerful tool in gathering information.

'Tell me why you want it redecorated' may elicit more than 'why do you want it redecorated?' It may seek out more of the rationale behind the decision and spark a desired outcome that would otherwise be missed. It makes it expressed rather than assumed or implied, and it tends to focus the mind on the future. It is, after all, in the future that the assessment of performance will take place. The latter question, however, tends to focus on the present or past and leads to a criticism of what needs to change. It may still be possible to ascertain desired outcomes from the question but it is not as likely to draw out positive expressions of what is wanted – rather, it will contribute to what is not wanted.

'Explain what constraints have to be imposed' goes even further into the reasons behind any constraints rather than simply identifying what they may be. If nothing else it also prompts the person initiating the activity to consider certain aspects more fully than they may otherwise have done.

'Describe what you will be looking for ...' immediately stimulates visual thinking and can help to identify some of the sources of evidence that show that the activity has been carried out to the required standard of performance.

As a leader we should be empowering our teams to request this information from us, or from anybody else for whom they carry out work. We should, of course, bear TED in mind to guide our own thinking so that everything that matters for an activity or role is clearly expressed in advance, leaving no surprises for later.

It is permissible to ask individuals or teams 'how would you go about achieving these outcomes?' and to guide their thinking. It would be disempowering, however, to tell them how to do it.

Back then to the redecorating. Having used TED, we may arrive at the following outcomes:

- the walls, ceiling, doors and window frames are cleanly finished in your chosen colours;
- there are no paint stains on furniture, fixtures or fittings;
- the carpet is not damaged;
- the materials and labour costs are within budget;

- no cracks or blemishes are visible;

- the job is completed by 5.00 pm on Friday, 4 November this year.

If all the above were then achieved, would it be appropriate to criticise the decorators if they hadn't repainted the radiators and removed them to clean and paint the wall behind? Inevitably there are occasions when unexpected issues will emerge: are you going to empower the decorators to deal with each one or are you going to empower them to come and ask you what you would prefer?

An outcome provides an objective measure that should not be open to misinterpretation. It removes subjective assessment and a collection of them indicates clearly all the significant factors that determine success. Contingency and 'what if' factors should also be considered at the outset. For example:

- If you empower a salesperson to bring in £10,000 of sales revenue, what if it costs the company £5,000 in the process?

- If you empower a computer programmer to design and install a particular computer program by a fixed date, what if another program crashes as a result?

- If you empower someone to service your car, what if they take two days when you wanted it back in one?

Many years ago I conducted a customer care assignment for a major computer mainframe manufacturer. This gave me the opportunity to visit a number of customers' sites where the field service engineers – my target group – were operating. There was one site in particular where there were three such engineers permanently on site to maintain the operation of the mainframe computer.

I spent some time with them and asked them how they measured their success – what did it look like when they were doing a good job? Almost in unison, and with a great sense of pride, they said that their job was to keep the mainframe up and running so that its 'downtime' was kept to a minimum – even if it meant replacing a worn belt-drive with a stocking while a replacement was ordered and delivered.

So I then had the opportunity to speak to their customer contact at the same head office site. When I asked him how he measured the success of the field service engineers who were responsible for maintaining and servicing the mainframe, his response was discouraging. He related how he was concerned that the time spent fixing problems was often not enough, and that he'd rather they took longer and did it properly. 'Can you believe', he mused, 'that they even put a stocking on the belt drive to get it up and running? That's no bloody good to me – if the mainframe goes down again during a payroll run, I'm b******d!'

When I then asked if he had expressed that to the engineers the answer was, 'not in so many words'.

It is not the number of words that matter. What does matter is that what is important is expressed – and expressed to the people performing the activity. It seemed that too much reliance was given here to the service level agreement (SLA), which neither the engineers nor this customer contact were involved in negotiating. The engineers believed they were doing the customer a favour by reducing downtime by whatever means. The customer didn't want a quick fix with a short life expectancy, he wanted a longer fix that would survive for longer. When I got the two parties to communicate with each other and agree their own outcomes, 99.9 per cent of the customer service issues were resolved. No longer did customers have to fit the SLA, the SLA fitted the customer.

Ambient leadership

Ambient leadership is that influenced by middle managers in their interpretation of policies and plans and the way they cascade these to their teams. It is more usually at this level that the burden of responsibility rests for implementing major change.

Whereas TED is a useful tool for clarification at a task level, the ambience of an organisation is affected by something more. Nothing affects morale more than employees feeling they are being imposed upon, taken for granted or ignored altogether. So what can leaders do to get them on their side? A tool not normally associated with empowerment is the 'art of selling', so let's explore how 'selling' affects empowerment.

Selling change

Having spent the early years of my professional career researching and designing sales training programmes before becoming more involved in management and latterly leadership development, I have seen what managers miss most. They lack the communication skills that become the bedrock of good sales technique.

Yet managers need to sell. It could be to sell why things won't happen as much as why there is a need for certain actions to be carried out. More than ever nowadays, what needs to be sold is change. The mistake often made is that managers 'tell' rather than 'sell', and they do so because they feel that the authority invested in them allows them to. They therefore also assume that staff have to listen and obey.

The stages of the 'sales cycle' are generally recognised as planning, prospecting, qualifying, needs development, objection handling and closing the sale. If we take a look at each of these we can see the relevance to leadership.

Planning

The plan here focuses on what it is that is being sold. What is the product or service going to be? Who are the people it would benefit, and how much will it cost?

Prospecting

A prospect is a potential buyer of the product or service. So this stage is concerned with trawling through directories and data banks to identify the names and contact details of the companies or individuals for whom the product or service is targeted.

Qualifying

This develops prospecting to the next level – taking the prospect beyond being merely a name and set of contact details. The aim is to find out more about the prospect's business and gather as much information as possible that may link your product or service to them. Contact may be made directly at this stage with the prospect, perhaps talking to anyone in that company other than the buyer. Information is then used to get that all important appointment. Likes, dislikes or attitude could be helpful to know, along with background to their company, customer base and current suppliers.

Needs development

This is where the sales interaction really begins. The sales person opens the discussion by drawing the buyer's attention to 'what's in it' for the buyer. The important lesson for all sales people is that we buy things not because of what they are but because of what they can do for us. They save us time, money or injury, give us status or security, or gain us time, money and enjoyment. The features only become relevant when we are first sold on the benefits of having them.

Imagine you are looking at a car in a showroom and are still undecided about what to buy. The salesperson may approach and ask you a few questions to establish what you may need. 'Are you looking for something for long journeys with the family's luggage or just a means for getting around town?' 'Which is more important to you – economy or comfort?'

The response to these questions will help to identify that you are looking for:

- something for long journeys that is comfortable with all the family's luggage;
- something just to get around town that is economical;
- something for long journeys that is economical;
- something just to get around town that is comfortable;
- something comfortable and economical for long and short journeys, and there's no family luggage to worry about.

There may be other variables too. Whatever the response a dialogue has been entered into and it's not so easy for you to avoid it by saying 'I'm just looking', the usual response to 'Can I help you?' Furthermore, a pathway has been established by the salesperson to identify the end product that you'll be satisfied with. In fact, if they are really skilled they may get you to acknowledge that you have a need for something that you hadn't previously thought of and for which you would be prepared to pay that little bit extra.

How do they do it? The skill is that they get you to make the decisions. They don't sell it to you: you sell it to yourself. They just help you along by asking relevant questions to differentiate between one car and the next. They know where the questions may be leading, though you may not.

Skilled salespeople will not tell you what to do with your money, but they may summarise the decisions you have made en route:

> 'So you're looking for something that is comfortable for long journeys, has a foldable rear seat to extend the luggage space when needed, will do around 34 mpg and has the additional feature of satellite navigation so you no longer waste time trying to find your destination. In that case, this is the car for you, wouldn't you agree?'
>
> 'Would you like it in this colour or is there another you prefer?'

By this stage you may no longer be debating whether you're going to buy the car: instead the focus has changed to the colour.

Objection handling

Were you to raise an objection a trained salesperson would be ready for it. The fact you've entered the showroom already suggests you have an interest in one or other of the cars on show. You may yet need to convince yourself, however.

Empathy has to be a trait of a good salesperson, because without it they can't see the other side of the transaction: seeing the product from the prospect's point of view, understanding and appreciating their concerns.

So you may even say 'I'm not sure £300 extra is worth it for satellite navigation.' To which the salesperson may enquire:

'Would it be worth less than £1 per day to you over the next year to avoid the frustration and wasted time of being lost near your destination? You suggested you'd be looking to have the car at least three years, so that's only less than 30p per day, plus you get the advantage of route planning too. Wouldn't you agree that's a benefit you can afford?'

Closing the sale

There are a number of techniques that can be used to close a sale – which means get the business or commitment. Two worth mentioning here in particular are the 'alternative' close and the 'summative' close, and we've seen examples of them above.

The 'summative' close summarises all the 'yes' or positive responses from the prospect and restates the product or service that offers these: 'So you're looking for something that is ... This is the car for you then, don't you agree?'

The 'alternative' close is a good appendage to the summative close because it can move the focus from the big decision (which car?) to a smaller one (which colour?) – having assumed the big decision is in the bag.

Other 'alternatives' could be: 'Would you like to pay cash or take advantage of our hire purchase plan?' 'Would you like it delivered or are you going to collect it?' 'Which suits you best, next week or the week after?'

Professional salespeople lead the sale. They know the product or service and they get to know the prospect. Asking questions shows an interest in the prospect, not the product. Telling the prospect about the products, however, before establishing whether a particular feature is of interest shows that the attention is on the product and not the prospect. Telling them is not selling them.

Professional salespeople create a vision for the prospect in which the prospect can see themselves already enjoying the prospective purchase. They provide an opportunity for any questions or concerns to be addressed so that the prospect can convince themselves they are doing the right thing. In effect, the prospect has been empowered by the salesperson – the prospect made the decision themselves! Their participation was controlled though they were free to respond how they wished.

Relevance to leadership

Shall we now get back to leading empowerment? If you need to say 'yes' then perhaps you're missing the point, because we've never left the topic. Substitute 'salesperson' for 'leader', 'prospect' for 'follower' and 'product or service' for 'task or activity'.

The subject matter will inevitably be different, yet the structure and techniques should not be. The sale is made when the followers are committed to working towards the agreed outcomes.

Planning

What is the task, activity or role, or change, going to look like? What resources are likely to be involved or affected?

Prospecting

Who may have the skills and knowledge to achieve the desired outcomes? Who may have the potential with a bit of help from training?

Qualifying

Find out more about the individuals before speaking to them. What might their attitudes be or previous experiences? What could they add to the activity?

Needs development

Is there a benefit for the individual or team that might get their attention or desire to know more? Are they going to increase their earnings or opportunities to earn more? Are they going to save effort or time that could be used to their benefit elsewhere? Will their status be enhanced? Can they save their business from going under and secure their jobs?

The essential aspect to bear in mind here is that individuals buy into something because of what benefit it gives them, not what it gives to someone else. A person doesn't buy a Ford or a Saab so that Ford and Saab can benefit from the sale. So why should you think followers will buy into an activity or change if the benefit you offer is that 'the company will make increased revenue' or 'the company's profit will improve' or the 'shareholders' dividend will increase in value'. Individuals will be asking, 'What's in it for me (WIIFM)?' – forget the company and the shareholders!

Objection handling

Anticipate likely questions, objections or concerns. Acknowledge the individual's or team's comments and restate the benefit. Put it into a daily, weekly or other context that magnifies the occasions on which benefit is gained. Offset a genuine issue that may be perceived as negative by compensating for it with the positives that are on offer.

It is also critical to speak the same language that the other person identifies with. As above, individuals will identify with money in their own pockets rather than money in the company's coffers; they will prefer to hear about time they are saving for themselves rather than efficiency gains for the organisation. They may also express particular terminology in their objection and this is the clue as to the level of language with which to continue the conversation. Acknowledge it rather than ignore it.

Closing the sale

After each objection, if any, has been acknowledged and addressed as above, summarise the positive responses and 'what's in it for them'. But don't do this unless the prospects have been involved in the foregoing discussions.

One thing to note is that salespeople deal with the future. They provide solutions to address your need, yet sometimes we don't actually know we have a need because we are not aware of the solution. We know the past and our experiences with it but we often require educating by the salesperson so that we have the knowledge to make the right decision that affects our future. The key is that successful salespeople generate the feeling that the prospect's need to buy is greater than the salesperson's need to sell.

They provide the bridge from the past to the future. If our needs are correctly expressed, and we have the money, we are likely to take that bridge. That may be the same bridge we will see later in the 'change model' and in each case we have to take ourselves across it, even though we may have to be led to do so.

So what is the 'money' in the context of our employer selling to us? What is it we need to have enough of? It could well still be money. If we feel we will be losing more than we gain, in relative value, we may prefer not to buy into the change. So money could translate into time.

It could also translate into recognition. Earlier we saw the significance of the factors that motivate individuals.

The 'alternative close' should be used carefully and positively. Using 'so do you want to keep your jobs or not?' would come across as more of a threat (however accurate the reality!). Instead, it requires an approach that moves the sale forward to a commitment. A better choice would be: 'So would you like to start on Monday at 9.00 am, or at 9.30 am?'

Organisational leadership

This focuses on the purpose, values, strategy and success model for the organisation.

Continuous improvement frameworks, involving representation from the spectrum of work disciplines, are essential empowerment tools at this level. These can work alongside tailored appraisal systems and performance management frameworks that are outcome-focused rather than input orientated.

Perhaps a criticism levelled at ISO standards is that they are very process-focused and bring about a consistency of performance. That performance, however, may consistently lead to a poor product or service.

Determining desirable outcomes, in the way this book provides examples, will promote better attention to quality. There should not be a place on appraisal forms for poor, below average, average, satisfactory, above average, exceptional or exceeds expectations. Their very presence suggests that they are allowed to exist and that quality is accepted as varying by degrees. Either people meet the standard or they don't – in which case look to help them as early as possible.

Empowerment makes quality non-negotiable.

Language and behaviour

Implementing an empowerment culture within your team or organisation is itself introducing change, though we might use empowerment to bring other changes about as shown in the case study in Chapter 7.

As we've seen on a few occasions in this book, empowerment necessitates some adjustment to the current language and behaviours so that the focus is on outcomes and not inputs, and so that leaders enable and let go rather than interfere. It is important to recognise the significance of language in selling change.

There is a body of work known as the LAB Profile, where LAB is an abbreviation for Language and Behaviour. This is a subsidiary framework to NLP (NeuroLinguistic Programming) and was developed by Rodger Bailey whose work is discussed further in Shelle Rose Charvet's book *Words That Change Minds* (1997). Charvet provides a more complete picture, but there are three patterns of motivational traits that are worth a mention here.

Based around 'Transformational Grammar',[1] these traits show how a person's experiences and make-up are revealed in language patterns and behaviour patterns, and learning to recognise them can help you predict and influence their behaviour. As with most analytical tools it has to be recognised that the patterns will relate to specific contexts, and may not represent an individual's behaviour were it to be in a different place, at a different time and with different people.

There are two distinct groups of traits covered: motivational traits and working traits. The motivational traits that are relevant indicate how people trigger and maintain their interest level and what will demotivate them. The three in particular to review here are the traits for 'direction', 'reason' and 'decision factors'.

Direction

Imagine a continuum of behaviour where at one extreme is exhibited a desire *towards* achieving a particular goal, while at the other is displayed a dissatisfaction and need to move *away from* the current situation.

Away from   Towards

The 'towards' person may desire things simply because they are worth having. They are centred on achievements but may, in their eagerness, fail to see obstacles in their way. They have a 'can do it now' attitude and see the positives in most things that they do see. Their energy is given to attainment and they may become demotivated where there is no goal for them to reach.

On the other hand, the 'away from' person focuses more on what is, or what may be, going wrong. Their motivation is to solve problems and their inclination towards a goal is so that they can get away from their current position where its disadvantages are becoming all too evident. However, the analyst and critic in this person's make-up will see the obstacles en route to the goal and this may inhibit progress towards it until they are fully considered and overcome.

Reason

As we know, there are people who seem happy to accept and follow procedures and yet others seem to rebel at the thought and are always looking for alternative routes. The trait here explores whether a person is the former or the latter.

Procedures   Options

Those who are more procedures orientated tend to speak in terms of procedures: 'the right way'; 'first ... secondly ...'; and they are more likely to relate information through a logical sequence of events or a series of chronological occurrences. They thrive on having a set path to follow and reaching the end of it.

Options people would frustrate procedures people and vice versa. Options people look for options – other ways of doing things – and are motivated by creativity.

Decision factors

This trait examines the extent to which a person reacts to change and the frequency of change they need.

There are those people who hate change and prefer regular routine; they want their world to stay the same and may only welcome change every twenty years or so. These are 'sameness' traits.

Then there are others who prefer things to evolve gradually over time, perhaps allowing significant change every five years or so. This reflects 'sameness with exception'.

If you want things to be drastically different, with major change every one or two years, you would be a 'difference' person, while there is also a 'sameness with exception and difference' trait for those who can accept radical change but who are comfortable allowing things to evolve. Change every three years would suffice.

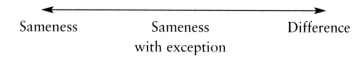

Sameness	Sameness with exception	Difference

It is more likely that people will show an inclination somewhere along each continuum above rather than be located at the extremes, but often a dominating trait will emerge.

So imagine an environment where the work is very routine and procedural but involves an element of problem-solving. What traits would it be preferable for those workers to have? Well, it would be fair to suggest that if they possessed traits weighted to the left side of each continuum they would suit the requirements of the role.

So picture the company employing dynamic, forward-thinking directors from outside to make the company more competitive and efficient, directors who have a track record of achievements and experience of new technology. Where might they sit on the scales?

Such a disparity of language nearly killed the change stone dead for a pensions administration company. Yes, the proposed change was necessary; the company needed to have a computerised framework to reduce paperwork and storage space, and speed up the service on member schemes. It was an exciting time for the directors but they initially failed to see that what motivated them was scary for the staff. While they would speak of 'remove and replace', 'radically different' and 'computerised systems being the way forward', the staff would be looking instead at the negatives and resisting the implementation of such revolutionary change.

The change model

The 'change model', which is an adaptation of Elisabeth Kübler-Ross's (1969) bereavement counselling model, identifies four stages which people go through when experiencing change (see Figure 5.2).

We all follow this route, though some may pass through it very quickly if they are choosing the change, and others may get stuck somewhere if the change is imposed on them. Even welcome change can leave you in denial, as it seems too good to be true and you're afraid it may just be a dream.

What does *denial* look like? Like people don't care, as apathy and numbness set in and little work gets done. You might hear them say 'It'll never happen!'

Resistance is to be expected then. This is the phase when we feel like rebelling. We get outside our comfort zone and can lash out at people, things, views and ideas with which

Figure 5.2   Stages of the change model (and team development)

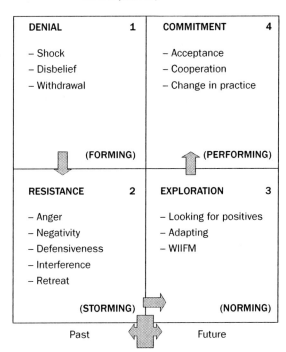

DENIAL 1	COMMITMENT 4
– Shock	– Acceptance
– Disbelief	– Cooperation
– Withdrawal	– Change in practice
(FORMING)	(PERFORMING)
RESISTANCE 2	EXPLORATION 3
– Anger	– Looking for positives
– Negativity	– Adapting
– Defensiveness	– WIIFM
– Interference	
– Retreat	
(STORMING)	(NORMING)

Past   Future

Source: Based on Kübler-Ross (1969).

we feel uncomfortable. All the anger that is felt by the peer group or individual comes to the surface, if the organisation allows it to. It is critically important to allow this to happen – let the bad out so that the good can get in.

Empowerment is also critical. You should empower those affected by the change to ask questions and express concerns. Better still, involve them through continuous improvement programmes or employee representation in early consultation to agree the need for change and propose options. At least by the time the change arrives it may be seen as more of an evolution than a revolution and pacify those sameness with exception people while gaining the approval of those with difference motivational traits. The change can then be sold rather than told.

The purpose of the change model is to manage expectations. We also manage expectations when we empower. Knowing there will be resistance is one thing, but stirring it up is another. In the example of the pensions administration company the directors needed to speak the same language as the staff. They needed to reassure them that 'the core of your jobs will remain the same but the computer can take over much of the mundane work, giving you more time for problem-solving and interfacing with client members'.

There was little change to the outcomes being sought but this needed restating. The methodology would be different for a number of activities but it was necessary to remind them of what would remain the same and to let them see the new procedure. The sooner they saw the procedure – even though it wouldn't be in operation for some time – the sooner they would want to follow it.

Suppressing resistance is not advised. It certainly isn't empowering and it will be like a time bomb waiting to explode. Such bombs have a tendency to go off when you least expect them to – so much for managing expectations when one does.

What does resistance look like? It can take the form of withdrawal from the team, depression, frustration, anger, stubbornness and constant sniping at the change. They say 'It'll never work!'

Exploration is the stage when one focuses on the positives rather than negatives – but only because the negatives have had their moments of expression. It's now time to reflect on what the future may look like, sound like and feel like in a positive light.

At some time there is a letting go, a saying goodbye to the past. While not forgetting, people may forgive or, at least, understand the reasons why the changes occurred or had to be made. In bereavement terms this could be seen as the wake. In the model it is a bridge between stage 2 and stage 3, and it's made of wood. Once you're over the bridge – having got yourself over it – there is no going back. You burn the bridge in your mind.

One company encouraged and paid for a good party at each location before a new amalgamated branch network was opened. Even those made redundant turned up and enjoyed the evening. The staff and management were told that this was part of the change process and how significant it was to have this 'bridge'. Those I spoke to at the locations where these parties occurred (fortunately not on the same night) confirmed that they could only look ahead now – and that included those who were redundant.

Communicating openly with all the people all the time cannot be underestimated. As with justice, it must not only be done but must be seen to be done.

Give them the knowledge. Treat them with respect and trust. Such evidence of a degree of humanity during the process destroys the platform for the negative opinion formers.

What does exploration look like? People show a renewed interest and exert more energy. They question more though there may even be some confusion as the old mixes with the new. They say 'How does this work?'

The bereavement model referred to stage 4 as acceptance. However, in leadership terms we are seeking more than acceptance: we want *commitment*. The former can be quite passive but we want action, and we want action that is supportive of the change.

What does commitment look like? Teamwork is more evident and people become more cooperative and act with more purpose than they may have done for a while. They say 'I'll do that'.

Note

1. 'Transformational Grammar' was a term coined by Noam Chomsky (a US linguist) who perceived that below the actual phrases and sentences of a language (the surface structure) there exists a more unconscious and basic layer (the deep structure) that is processed by various rules as we speak them or write them. There is therefore a system of formal rules on how we transform them from a deep to a surface structure.

6

Monitoring the cultural change and dealing with feedback

Taking a sound reading

If empowerment has been implemented properly, not only should tasks and activities have descriptions of what they look like when they are done well, so should the entire empowerment culture. With the culture, we can go a step further and describe what it sounds like, as hinted in Chapter 1.

Monitoring of anything is difficult to do well if there are no measures in place. And to monitor consistently using two or more people it is essential that the measures are objective and not subjective. It also helps if you provide the platform for drawing out indicators of the change.

One organisation had boasted in its company mission and values that it empowers its staff. When it took over a sizeable IT operation it was still making such boasts after two years. My involvement with them came about when I was invited to tender for a programme targeted at first-line managers to address the fact that they were not communicating up the line enough, despite the channel in the opposite direction being well used.

This really needed investigating before a solution could be proposed so I was granted the opportunity to talk to key members of the target group and to one or two of the managers to whom they reported. What began to emerge was a tale of suppression, distrust, resentment and bewilderment. It became clear that a much wider cultural issue was at play which could only be resolved by addressing it with all the staff on site, and that included the local equivalent to the managing director and the board.

Through a structured series of programmes, starting with the first-line managers through to the board, perceptions were passed up the line with the permission of each group. The company that liked to use the empowerment word at the time were, for the first time at this location, putting an ear to the ground.

Below is a selection of comments from the initial two-day programmes or the follow-up days. In each case the comment represents more than one voice and was given in response to the learning points of the programme, particularly regarding communication and empowerment. Delegates were happy for their comments to be valued but, because of CLMs (career limiting moves), names were not attributed. (A fuller listing of the comments received is given in Appendix 4.)

Communication downwards considered, but not upwards.

They encourage you to speak out, but the reactions when you do show that it's not advisable.

There is a perception that 'we' were bad and 'they' are good.

Don't waste time on contractors whose knowledge may be lost as soon as they leave.

There is a lack of opportunity to extend technical skill and little investment in training and development.

Impossible deadlines are usually set without consultation.

Feel that we're moving forward but dragging bits of the past along – pensions, contracts, etc.

The closure of the *xyz* office was reported in *Computer Weekly* before staff there were informed by the company.

We knew he wouldn't turn up – he's a busy man and we're not that important.

When all the comments were gathered, it was the board's turn to attend the programme. Whereas other programmes used a simulated case study to draw out learning, the board were presented with the comments and asked to categorise them in whatever way they saw fit and to produce an action plan for addressing each issue raised.

Acting on feedback

All credit to them, they had accepted the earlier investigation and recommendation to provide a solution that addressed the wider issue and not merely a symptom of it. Having invested in that they knew there would be some feedback that they might find unpalatable. They were nonetheless shocked to discover a language they didn't know existed within the site. They had not heard the term CLM before and were further surprised to learn that the previous employers had not communicated news of the impending takeover to its employees. One day they worked for one company, and the next day for another. No wonder the language indicated that people were in denial and resistance. The 'we' and 'them' attitude was worse than they had thought.

The board classified six key areas that would be given their attention. They set out realistic deadlines to accomplish actions under each classification, and no deadline was further than three months away. Each board member took responsibility for achieving the new vision through applying what they had learned and seeking the support of staff. Going straight out and empowering them was not likely to work without first gaining trust and respect for each other, as was identified in Chapter 4. The board had included itself in the development programme but still had to demonstrate that it was a part of the solution too.

The plan had the following classifications and action points:

- *Office structure*:
  - Reorganise the office layout
- *Evaluation process*:
  - Review the appraisal framework
  - Review objective setting
  - Review how improvements are measured
- *Time management*:
  - Review priorities to make time for interventions with staff
- *Communication strategies*:
  - Clarify objectives of *abc*
  - Organise communication and social events

- – Communicate 'empowerment' to *all* staff
- – Instigate and support team briefings
- – Develop a framework for running effective meetings
- *Empowerment*:
  - – Identify how to make people feel valued
  - – Allocate staff appropriately to projects
  - – Develop coaching skills within management
  - – Identify appropriate uses of delegation
  - – Roll out the management development programme to other sites
  - – Empower staff with questioning skills
- *Processes*:
  - – Explore the application and implementation of quality circles
  - – Protect staff from changing priorities
  - – Review processes with a view to improving the service to the client

Nearly all these actions were completed within the timescale, and those that had not met the deadline were seen to be works in progress.

The true measure of the success of the new culture occurred about a month before the overall deadline. The organisation is run by partners to whom the local 'managing director' reports. Previously it was well-known when the MD had been visited by a partner because, having usually been given 'the jackboot', he would come out of his office and kick everyone else! After such a visit one day, everyone prepared themselves for some seat of the pants motivation. But it didn't happen.

Instead, the MD called a meeting of senior management and outlined the purpose of the visit. He didn't blame, didn't criticise and didn't dictate. He put to them a vision of what something needed to look like and asked for their help. From that moment there was known to be a new 'them'. The site was united in its values and vision and the talk was at last being walked. Some respect was shown and reciprocated and the entire site was the new 'we'. Unfortunately it was the partners who had earned the label 'them'.

Compliance

The foregoing example bears out further thinking on motivation. Regarded as the three Cs of motivation, there are three methods of gaining compliance: coercive, calculative and cooperative.

Coercive compliance uses threats. It appeals to one's sense of fear and may gain results in the short term but, in the longer term, it will create resentment and possibly lead to sabotage or desertion.

Calculative compliance uses rewards. It calculates that if x is provided then it may be possible to get workers to attain y, as in incentive schemes. It appeals to one's sense of greed more than accomplishment. Again it may pay in the short term but it breeds an 'expectant' culture where they would always expect some additional reward to get work done, occasionally holding you to ransom if necessary.

Cooperative compliance, however, uses knowledge and shared information. It appeals to one's sense of ownership and esteem and demonstrates how much you value the individual. In the short term it promotes shared responsibility and commitment and gets results. In the longer term it breeds loyalty.

Perhaps they best differentiate between an empowerment approach and other approaches. The cooperative style is very much the same as empowerment. The power to perform is achieved through the acquisition or sharing of knowledge. The knowledge is brainpower once again. The organisation above had been preaching empowerment but not seeking cooperative compliance: it had a tendency towards coercion instead. One major lesson learned in that environment was that if you use threats and appeal to fear or disrespect people, they will put you in the proverbial. If you respect their abilities and truly empower them, they can help you out of it! And if you'd started out empowering, using open communication and measurable signposts en route, you may never have got in it in the first place.

It is imperative that regular monitoring is carried out and that realistic deadlines are set which should not be missed without valid reason. Remember there are excuses that sound good, but only good sound excuses are permitted.

Whereas empowerment has been chosen as an organisational style it should be backed up with enabling programmes. Attendance itself should be monitored so that no one escapes the net.

Managers and leaders who have been enabled with tools like Johari and the empowerment window, the enabling cocktail (Martini glass) and how to express outcomes should be receiving regular attention from their own managers. They should be asked what decisions the team has been allowed to make that would have an impact on them. How has openness within the team been achieved? And what steps have been taken to establish the strengths and weaknesses of team members?

Whereas the implementation phase sets out what empowerment would look like when it is done well within the organisation, feedback should focus on the evidence suggested by the outcomes – the look, sound and feel factors. A gap analysis, every month or quarter, with reviewed action plans will keep the attention where it is required. The adage 'what gets measured gets done' only applies realistically when someone knows it's going to be checked. And it is checked when it matters.

Culture vs nationality

There is, of course, another interpretation of what is meant by 'culture'.

Culture and nationality should not be confused. Nationality categorises an individual as belonging to a particular country, where by virtue of that country the individual may be perceived to possess certain traits (e.g. the British 'stiff upper lip', the Italian penchant for gesturing with the hands, the Japanese humility). Nationality suggests characteristics. Culture, on the other hand, goes much deeper. It reflects beliefs. Culture can be described as a shared set of values and basic tacit assumptions that determine a group's perceptions, thoughts, feelings and behaviour. So while a nation may indeed exhibit an outward sign of culture, there will be underlying subcultures exhibited by the diverse pockets of individuals that make up the nation. Such a pocket is likely to prevail within any given corporation.

There is a school of thought that takes the view that corporations assume a personality, that in effect they can be people too. This stems from the image they project to the world, an image which their customers or clients buy into and which, for all intents and purposes, is looking to reflect back to those same customers and clients a set of shared values. Thus Nike sought to reflect the aspirations of sporting winners before targeting a fashion conscious youth culture with its 'Just Do It' campaign. A winning image for winners followed by a trendy image for the fashionable. When, however, the company became embroiled in claims of using slave labour in Asia, the image the world then saw was an uncaring one showing little respect for its fellow man. Sales dropped and Nike was forced to address its failings and to reinstate and actually live to a set of values more acceptable to its target market.

The message for today's world is clear. Consumers buy into the association of a product or service with their own standards or ideals. The company therefore exhibits a personality. Companies really can be people too.

What is the relevance when considering empowerment? The simple answer is that empowerment should not be allowed to undermine a desirable set of values. When Nike empowered its business partners to come up with end products, it turned a blind eye to how they achieved their objectives. Nike then suffered by becoming associated, however unwittingly, with the negative aspect of a follower's methodology. Happily, recognition of this impact enabled Nike to eventually turn itself around.

In a globalised economy, cultural awareness is a 'must have'. Management today necessitates understanding one's own culture in the context of another. We cannot simply change our beliefs, but we can develop an awareness of how different sets of values might interact. The aspiring European who begins to lead a group of Asians by shouting, losing his temper and generally humiliating them will already have 'lost face' with his followers. That style might work in the West, but it is likely to lead to failure in the East ... and one never gets a second chance to make a first impression.

Cultural distance

Cultural distance then is the extent to which the set of values and behavioural norms of one group differs from another. In business this has long been interpreted as being due to national characteristics, but national boundaries are becoming continually eroded by globalisation. This occurs through cross-border mergers and acquisitions, through emigration and immigration and by a level of education and media reach that sees youngsters in distant emerging markets experience the same MTV as their counterparts in the industrialised world. This was underlined in 2005 by news that recent research (Fang, forthcoming) shows a marked change in perceptions of national stereotypes from those proffered by Geert Hofstede in 1983. Precise details are not yet available from the new study but it should come as no surprise.

Hofstede identified four cultural dimensions to explain the behaviours of different national cultures. This enabled him to plot 50 countries and three regions along an Individualism Index and a Power Distance Index to reflect the extent to which individualism or collectivism held sway, and the degree to which individuals accepted authority without question or preferred more independence and consultation.

At that time, Asian and Latin American countries dominated in the grid for low individualism (= high collectivism) and significant acceptance of authority. Europe, North America and Australasia mapped into high individualism (= low collectivism) and greater independence from authority. This clustering by region reinforced the notion of 'Western' versus 'Asian' or 'Latin' stereotypes and has influenced opinion ever since.

The other two dimensions, when similarly mapped, showed an Uncertainty Avoidance Index against a Masculinity Index. This reflected the extent to which national culture determined the need to limit uncertainty (when threatened by ambiguous situations) and to what degree society's values were dominated by 'success, money, and things' (masculinity) versus 'caring for others and the quality of life' (femininity). Here the pattern was much less clustered by region, suggesting influences which extend beyond those that rub off from our neighbours. What were these influences? Hofstede doesn't say. Perhaps some countries had greater access to popular culture via the movies and had been affected accordingly?

Whatever the case twenty years ago, it seems that the old stereotypes are no longer valid. The British are apparently no longer seen as polite, bowler-hatted gentlemen and brolly-carrying ladies but are more associated with the other end of the spectrum ... no doubt due to the much publicised antics of a rude, binge-drinking culture that seems to surface on summer holidays abroad and at international football matches. The once famous British reserve seems to have been washed away by alcohol. Does this mean that Britain as a whole is a nation of yobbish alcoholics? Hopefully not. But perceptions do matter. And that is the point of any attempt to lead or manage across borders, because how we perceive others will influence our choice of attitude and language while how others perceive us will influence their reactions.

I can draw on my personal experiences of training people from different cultures and have heard the experiences of my family and friends who have worked for British, American, Canadian, Israeli, French, Swiss and Dutch companies in the UK, continental Europe and Asia Pacific. Even participating in full-time education with 33 different nationalities bears the same message. The one overriding revelation is that each has its own way of doing things. There may be similarities, but these will be characterised by their differences. The methodology may be the same, but the time taken to deliberate and indeed the people who should deliberate – based on cultural hierarchies – would be different. Words like 'must', 'ought to' and 'should' might be replaced by 'be nice to', 'would like you to' and 'probably be better if'. Tone of language is a tool to be used to achieve an effect. Get it wrong, and you achieve nothing.

Allowances should be made for national language interpretations. While the English use the word 'special' in a positive sense (above average, exceptional), the French use it negatively (peculiar, difficult). So the 'special' employee is likely to be favoured in an Anglo-Saxon environment, but shunned in a French one. Imagine then the impact of an English boss proudly telling his French employees how 'special' they are!! The disappointment will be etched on their faces.

By the same token, language difficulties can arise for a less obvious reason, as the discussion of the LAB profile shows in the previous chapter.

For some further guidelines on what empowerment within your team or organisation should look like, refer to the empowerment audit given in Appendix 3.

7

Case studies from the public and private sectors

The public and private sectors are distinguished from each other merely by the role money plays. Otherwise their mechanisms are very similar, requiring leaders to set out the vision and employees to carry it out, frequently under the watchful gaze of managers.

We therefore separate the two sectors more for ease of reference than anything else.

Public sector

The directors of a Housing Association based on England's South Coast saw the need to prepare for impending change. The countdown had begun on a likely merger with a locally based partner association and attention was going to need to be directed at preparing the management team. Being part of a bigger group would enable them to continue growing, creating more affordable homes, improving their services and maintaining their position as an important community regeneration agency in the area.

They had decided that it was essential to get the support of the management team and workforce if the merger was to be a success. So they instigated a 'Management Challenge' programme that provided leadership and management development through a series of tailored modules. Furthermore, they included themselves in the programme.

Up until this point there had been very little internally focused training for management. Individuals had been sponsored to attend development activities outside the organisation but the learning was not necessarily immediately applicable to their work environment. What is more, it was not a shared experience within the workplace.

The Management Challenge focused on the key topics and content below:

- Session 1: *Motivation*
  - Methods adopted currently to motivate staff
  - Beliefs regarding staff motivation
  - Methods adopted to deal with poor motivation
  - Application of motivational methods to meet different needs
  - Self-motivation – current approaches
  - Link between staff motivation and achievement of business outcomes
  - How staff are motivated to work in a dynamic and changing environment

- Session 2: *Empowerment*
  - Understanding the term 'empowerment'
  - Ways in which staff are currently empowered
  - Beliefs about empowerment and its impact on staff and organisational achievement and performance
  - Empowering groups and individuals – attitudes to letting go
  - Empowering in a dynamic and changing environment

- Session 3: *Team building*
  - Understanding methods of team working
  - Current knowledge and understanding of own team strengths and development needs
  - Beliefs about teamwork and its contribution to staff and organisational achievement
  - Personal roles in team building
  - Motivating teams to work in a changing environment

- Session 4: *Objective setting*
  - Current style of objective setting
  - Approach to agreeing, defining and measuring objectives
  - Understanding types of objective and how they affect individual, team and business performance

- Session 5: *Performance management*
  - Attitude to managing good and poor performance of individuals
  - Beliefs about the interaction of individual, team and organisational performance
  - Current approach and methods of applying tools from earlier sessions to manage performance
  - Understanding change management models and their role in performance management

The sequence of modules was the same for each management group, though the directors attended first together followed by the senior management team then first-line managers.

The modules had been identified from initial discussions with the HR manager and through the use of 360° feedback forms. These asked specific questions about the manager to which a positive or a negative response was indicated anonymously by their team member. An aggregate of the scores for each question highlighted the extent to which the subject matter of the question was a development issue for the manager.

Common feedback from 'followers' was that managers didn't display much trust in the abilities of their team and needed to let go more. Staff didn't feel consulted on issues on which they felt they had something to offer. It was almost as if the managers believed they had to have the answers themselves, as that was what they were paid to produce. Even team briefings were a rarity.

To a great extent this reflected the style of the directors too. They each had particular skills relevant to functional and technical expertise, but had mixed abilities as communicators and motivators. The chief executive was quite a strong character who perhaps intimidated the views of his fellow directors without intending to. His 'shaper' tendencies would take over. Instead of encouraging open discussion, his opinions and ideas were sometimes hard to challenge without appearing to question his judgement or position. He was nonetheless very likeable.

The directors' style had a knock-on effect down the line. At the outset of the Management Challenge the Association looked like this:

- Orders were often given without explanation.
- Praise or recognition of routine achievement was very rare.
- Staff would be told what to do.
- Team briefings and consultations were not happening for most of the departments.

- Focus was on tasks being designated, many of which lacked any objective measurement.

- Little was known about individuals in the working team and work was often assigned which was inappropriate to an individual's abilities.

- Rumours were rife and, in the absence of 'company feedback', the grapevine grew out of control.

The Association was nonetheless successful, but it wasn't realising its full potential and the impact of the merger was a major uncertainty over which it needed some control.

When the subject of empowerment was tackled with the directors, they recognised that it would provide the change they wanted, but that they were not readily equipped to bring it about. In fact, we spent longer, at their request, identifying the extent to which they empowered or disempowered, and exploring what the vision throughout should be. They needed to be enabled.

It soon became apparent to them that here was a great opportunity to involve staff, to allow them to participate in creating the new visions throughout the Association. The annual staff conference was a month away and it was decided to share with them what information was currently known about the merger – as staff believed they were being kept in the dark deliberately – and to instigate structured input from the staff regarding their own vision. After all, the majority had responded openly when asked to complete and submit the 360° feedback questionnaire.

The invitation to staff to provide input was initially met with scepticism and surprise – they had not participated in the conference before but just turned up and listened before enjoying the Association's hospitality. The comment was made that maybe the staff conference might have some staff input for a change rather than just management's.

Once staff teams got down to discussing issues in preparation for the big day, describing their vision for their team and the Association as a whole, a new unity and sense of shared ownership came out on display. They had been equipped with the tool to describe what it looks like, sounds like and feels like. Hence they contrasted the current look, sound and feel with what they would like each to be.

Sadly, though, insufficient time had been allocated on the day to present and review the many team contributions, only one of which was put forward by a director-led team. Frustration and a sense of betrayal crept in. Despite the good intent, the directors were judged instead on their actions, or lack of them.

Fortunately, the Management Challenge had also brought about a new openness of communication through the management levels and a common language of leadership. The directors' mistake was clearly pointed out to them and acknowledged by them. They then set another time for the staff input to be presented, reviewed and actioned where appropriate. It may not have been ideal for everyone, as some staff were not all available at the time, but a new culture was beginning.

The theme of performance management, in particular, no longer became the domain of senior management who would then impose a mix of subjective and objective measures. Instead, all management levels were invited to participate in formulating the business plan, having been enabled with outcome and objective-setting techniques and questioning skills. Key objectives were devolved to staff so they could agree on the outcomes that supported each one.

Once the new picture emerged, having empowered staff to reach agreement related to their functional areas, a new level of commitment was attained.

Examples of the Association's aims and key objectives are given below.

Aims:

- To be the local landlord of choice.

- To bring all homes requiring major repair up to modern standards.

- To provide 639 general needs and 378 shared-ownership good-quality homes within five years.

- To be recognised as a leading regeneration agency in the South of the country.

- To keep our finances strong.

Objectives:

- To deliver high-quality services to meet our customer needs and aspirations.

- To maintain low-cost homes that meet customer aspirations and increase asset value.

- To meet the housing needs of people on low incomes.

- To improve the capability, power and resources of local disadvantaged communities.

Previously, these were all that existed, lacking in objective measurement and failing to offer something with which staff could identify. If they don't know what the end result looks like, how will they know when they've arrived?

For each objective the functional teams then explored what they believed it would look like. The following outcomes were then described under each objective.

- *To deliver high-quality services to meet our customer needs and aspirations:*
  - 99 per cent of emergency and 98 per cent of urgent and routine repairs are completed within our published time-scales by January 2006.
  - A customer satisfaction level of 85 per cent (as measured by the status survey for overall satisfaction with landlord service) is achieved by March 2006.
  - Annual budget is not exceeded, or where extra funding is required appropriate authority is sought and confirmed before further expenditure is incurred.
  - Lettings are achieved to minority groups in proportion to their representation in the local authority housing registers by January 2004.
  - 75 per cent of all homes are let on first offer by December 2005.
  - The number of tenants leaving our properties for positive reasons is increased by 20 per cent by January 2008.

- *To maintain low-cost homes that meet customer aspirations and increase asset value:*
  - Major repairs are undertaken so that all properties meet the Decent Homes Standards by January 2008.
  - Procurement of lease properties, or those for purchase, meet the Decent Homes Standards at the time of procurement.
  - The average SAP (Standard Assessment Procedure for measuring energy efficiency) rating of general needs properties is improved by ten points over the next five years.
  - Inspections are carried out by 'qualified' personnel against specific criteria from the Decent Homes

Standards, and decisions on viability are based on these inspection reports.

- Landlords are consulted on action for major and minor repairs in advance and specifications are agreed with them.

- *To meet the housing needs of people on low incomes:*

  - All new homes are developed to achieve a minimum HQI (Housing Quality Indicator) score of 70 per cent by January 2008. (This is an analysis of each scheme based on criteria relating to room sizes, position, proximity to amenities, etc.)

  - Excellence in design achieves a tenant satisfaction rating of 95 per cent by January 2008.

  - Initial shares of 25 per cent are offered on all new shared ownership schemes by June 2006.

  - 25 per cent of the development programme is achieved by modular construction by 2008.

- *To improve the capability, power and resources of local disadvantaged communities:*

  - One new social economy business is developed which tackles social exclusion by 2008.

  - Policy responses to at least one social exclusion issue are identified and promoted each year.

  - A sustainability index is developed by 2004 to enable us to target services that will improve the communities where our tenants live.

  - The development of five additional resident groups is supported by December 2006.

  - IIC (Investors in Communities) accreditation is achieved by 2004. (This has since been superseded by 'In Business for Neighbourhoods'.)

The maxim 'what gets measured gets done' is bringing new direction and empowerment to this Housing Association. And it was all achieved by involving staff as early as possible and then being seen to take action. Feedback questionnaires were initially dismissed as going through the motions until action was seen to be taken on them. Devolving the formulation of the business plan to the functional teams not only applied empowerment practice, it also provided a platform to which staff were very much committed. Having set the mission themselves, they now wanted to get themselves there.

Private sector

A tale of two cities

In the Global Trade Finance Department of a leading international bank they used to say that 'individually we are quite smart, but collectively we are a genius'!

It was no idle boast. They had catapulted from humble beginnings to be a global leader in their field, heralded for their professionalism and innovation. They were a composite of diverse experiences and skill sets from different backgrounds brought together by the institution's desire to succeed. Nothing new in that.

However, in another institution with a similar composite and institutional desire, the outcome was very different.

Why? Leadership.

The successful group shared the compelling vision of its leader. He laid out his plans for all to hear and contribute to. He never interfered as a doer, but ensured he surrounded himself with exceptional people and worked diligently to promote the group, facilitate them towards their objectives and enable them to carry out their designated tasks. He gave credit where credit was due, quietly chastised wherever it was warranted, and fostered a culture of openness, professionalism and – unashamedly – fun. He didn't command their respect. He earned it.

The faltering group on the other hand was led by a leader who, if he had a vision, kept it to himself. He culled a pool of proven professionals by whom he felt threatened to surround himself with allies whose potential was greater than their proof. His mantra was (and still is) 'if you're not with me you're against me, and if you're against me you're out'. Constructive challenge and collaborative discussion were not encouraged. Having himself little experience of the field he had been appointed to lead, he nonetheless brought in a senior team of political appointees to foster his links to the well connected ... with costly consequences. He has fostered a closed culture, putting people on their guard rather than at ease. He is swift to publicly chastise, ready to take credit but not so keen to give it. He commands respect but doesn't deserve it.

Two leaders, similar resources, two very different outcomes – the willingness and ability of each to empower being the critical difference.

Acknowledging culture

While empowerment may be a desired goal, not everyone is ready for it.

While working in Singapore, a leader sought to give more autonomy to his team of five local girls to enable them to work less restrictedly and to free him up from having to micro-manage. The response surprised him. Only one of the girls accepted the increased responsibility, the others protested, saying 'but you're the boss ... the boss takes responsibility, that's what you're for!' They had seen empowerment as him abrogating his responsibility and dumping it on them. It didn't matter that he confirmed his overall responsibility was not being diminished. They had not signed up to make their own decisions. That was his job.

Quite simply their background and training had not equipped them for what was being proposed. This is no slur on them or Singapore, but a simple fact. Indeed, during that time the bank's Human Resources department expended much effort on encouraging more initiative and entrepreneurial drive among the local staff. Prizes were awarded for improving systems and processes. Held back by the Chinese proverb which cautions 'the nail whose head sticks up gets hit with a hammer', it was at first a struggle to get things rolling and suggestions were initially anonymous. However, once those suggestions were seen to be lauded by senior management and genuine cost-savings were made, the proposers came forward to claim their reward. No hammer on the head – a pat on the back maybe ... and the appreciation of their colleagues.

The lesson is that empowerment is contextual. Employees need to feel empowered, not put upon. Without enabling, empowerment simply doesn't happen. Cultural barriers need to be overcome with the carrot not the stick. Telling employees to feel empowered doesn't cut it. Empowerment has to be felt and accepted within.

Changing tack

Some more lead a ship! Preparing for the 2005–06 Clipper Round the World Yacht Race recently has provided some valuable lessons in empowerment.

The skippers for this race were all professional while the crews were a motley collective of 'did a flotilla in the Med once', 'had dinghy lessons when I was eight' or 'never set foot on a boat before'. While some very good training was given to all, the rate of absorption and application by the individual crew members was quite mixed ... and the only way a skipper got to know their competence was to get them to try a few manoeuvres.

It went like this:

> 'Aidy Boy, I want you to organise a starboard pole/port hoist for the spinnaker. You've got two minutes to organise your crew. Away you go.'
>
> 'Er, starboard pole/port hoist ... I'm not sure what you mean. Do we carry the starboard pole over to port and hoist it there, or are we hoisting the starboard pole to starboard but raising the spinnaker on the port side?'
>
> 'What do you think?'
>
> 'Er, the latter?!'
>
> Without further prompting or advice from the skipper, Aidy Boy assembles the crew with the plea, 'Okay, who's done this before then?' Blank looks.
>
> 'Your two minutes are up. You've got three to get started and finish it.'
>
> Flustered crewmembers are appointed to respective tasks (uphaul, downhaul, guy, halyard, deck crew, pulpit, etc.). 'Everyone know what they're doing?'
>
> 'No.'

The next five minutes was a shambles of coordination, yelling by too many chiefs and a loss of control which nearly catapulted the pulpit crew into the water. They were very much 'all at sea'.

The problem was that neither Aidy Boy nor the rest of the crew could visualise the objective. They weren't certain of the intended outcome and even though they guessed correctly, carrying it out was frustrated by a lack of experience and competence.

Picture the scene then some months later once the skipper had shared his vision of every evolution on the yacht and gone through each several times to embed crew awareness. That same pole hoist took one minute and fifteen seconds in virtual silence. All crew knew their stations, and each also knew how his or her role interacted with everyone else's. A silent evolution is the hallmark of a competent crew.

So, 'lead a ship'. Empowerment, too, makes use of a natural resource and, when correctly applied, it won't take the wind out of your sails.

Appendix 1
Leading the empowerment process

Characteristics of an empowered leader

Below is a list of characteristics that are said to describe the empowered leader.

Rank the characteristics in order of priority. Once you have done this, compare your ranking with those of your team and agree a team ranking.

Characteristics	Your ranking	Your team's ranking
1. Provider of a vision for the future		
2. Motivator		
3. Respects others		
4. Forms good working relationships		
5. Has strong interpersonal skills		
6. Is a strong communicator		
7. Acts as a coach and mentor		
8. Clarifies objectives		
9. Sees the customer as most important		
10. Describes behaviour in feedback		
11. Devolves responsibility		

Appendix 2
Job profile:
Head of Site Services

Reporting to: General Operations Manager

Role: To provide leadership and professional support to the company management team for AB&C hospitals

Responsibilities: All portering and domestic staff and service assets and the provision of cleaning and portering services delivery across the NHS Trust contract.

Direct: Domestic services – A&B hospitals only

Porter services – all hospitals, to include post, waste disposal and movement of patients, bodies, furniture and goods

Subcontractor: Grounds and gardens

Pest control   } – A&C hospitals only

Window cleaning

Key result areas	Sources of evidence	Skills and knowledge
Planning and organising		
■ An effective facilities management strategy is developed and implemented to deliver value-for-money services	■ Strategy document	■ Planning and analytical skills ■ Writing skills ■ Business objectives and service levels
■ Plans contribute to business objectives within the parameters of the client brief and Health & Safety legislation	■ Service level agreement ■ Site inspection reports	■ Health & Safety legislation ■ COSSH
■ Systems are established and applied to monitor and evaluate the quality and cost-effectiveness of services	■ 'System' documentation ■ Staff feedback ■ Action plans	■ Performance assessment ■ Cost control techniques ■ Performance standards
■ Providers of contracted services are selected and briefed to meet the relevant performance standards	■ Contractor records ■ Performance standards	■ Performance standards ■ Internal vs external resources
■ Workloads are anticipated and resources scheduled to meet predetermined service levels	■ Activity forecasts	■ Project management
■ Any unexpected shortfalls in resources are referred to the appropriate authority without undue delay	■ 'Authority' feedback ■ Customer feedback	■ Levels of authority and escalation procedure

Key result areas	Sources of evidence	Skills and knowledge
Planning and organising (cont'd)		
■ Risk assessments are carried out for all activities	■ Risk assessment reports	■ Risk assessment
■ Staff and non-staff budgets for site services are managed within their cash limits and comply with the company's financial instructions	■ Budget documentation ■ Company feedback	■ Budgeting and financial awareness ■ Company financial instructions
■ Safe working methods are defined and applied for all mechanical, electrical and manually operated equipment, and regular servicing and maintenance of all such equipment is planned and implemented	■ Planned maintenance agreements ■ Procedure manuals ■ Induction records ■ Observation of staff	■ Safe working practices ■ Planned maintenance strategies ■ Developing procedural documentation
■ Existing pest control arrangements are monitored and enforced regularly in all areas of responsibility	■ Work instruction notices ■ Inspection records ■ Environmental Health Authority	■ Pest control guidelines ■ Inspection procedures
■ Minimum standards are defined in purchasing contracts for all categories of equipment, disposables and cleaning chemicals	■ Purchasing contract records	■ Cost control techniques

Key result areas	Sources of evidence	Skills and knowledge
Leadership		
■ The company's vision, mission and values are communicated and adhered to by all staff	■ Minutes of staff briefings ■ Staff appraisal records ■ Customer and staff feedback	■ Vision, mission and values ■ Presentation techniques
■ The need for professional support is identified and given to operational managers where appropriate to achieve business objectives	■ 'Supervision' records ■ Feedback from operational managers ■ Performance against delivery standards	■ Business objectives ■ Development needs analysis ■ Coaching skills
■ Trust is shown in the abilities of staff and differences in opinions, attitudes or behaviours are addressed while respecting their dignity	■ Staff feedback ■ Disciplinary records ■ Formal/informal records	■ Interpersonal skills ■ Empowerment techniques
■ Advice and support is readily available and accessible to operational managers when requested	■ Staff feedback	■ Time management ■ Counselling skills
■ Health & Safety procedures and statutory requirements are maintained in accordance with company policy	■ Site inspection reports ■ Minutes of team meetings	■ Health & Safety legislation ■ Company policy ■ COSSH

Key result areas	Sources of evidence	Skills and knowledge
Customer interface		
■ The different customers in the Health Trust are identified and contact is made and regularly maintained to develop a working relationship with them	■ Health Trust organisation chart ■ Diary records ■ Correspondence	■ Interpersonal skills ■ Time management
■ Complex or high-profile customer problems are resolved without undue delay in agreement with the customer	■ The weekly activity report ■ Customer records fully completed	■ Negotiation skills
■ Transactions with external and internal customers comply with the company's vision, mission and values	■ Customer feedback	■ Vision, mission and values
■ External customer needs are regularly reviewed and acted upon in agreement with the customer	■ Minutes of meetings ■ Service delivery plans	■ Meetings management ■ Objective setting
■ Frequent 'walkrounds' are conducted at each site and any remedial action initiated in accordance with agreed procedures	■ Site survey reports ■ Customer feedback ■ Staff feedback	■ Performance standards ■ Agreed procedures ■ Site layout

Key result areas	Sources of evidence	Skills and knowledge
Reporting		
■ Mechanisms are in place, and are used regularly, for identifying and reporting on the financial spend for delivery of services	■ Budgets ■ Contract review documentation	■ Use of budgeting tools ■ Financial awareness
■ Mechanisms are in place, and regularly used, to identify compliance with company quality assurance systems	■ Reviews against delivery plans	■ Company quality assurance systems ■ Monitoring techniques
■ Staff meetings are held at least monthly across the services at which staff are kept up to date with local and wider company matters	■ Minutes of meetings ■ Staff feedback	■ Meetings management ■ Presentation techniques ■ Up-to-date company knowledge
■ All customer records are kept accurate, complete and up to date, and are readily available to authorised personnel	■ Customer database ■ Minutes of client meetings ■ Contract records	■ Company record systems ■ Levels of authority
■ All accidents and incidents are reported in accordance with company procedure	■ Health & Safety records ■ Accident reports ■ Customer and staff feedback	■ Health & Safety legislation ■ Company reporting procedures

Key result areas	Sources of evidence	Skills and knowledge
Training and development		
■ Competent individuals are assigned to demonstrate the correct procedures and impart relevant knowledge	■ Personal records ■ Certificates of competence	■ Correct procedures ■ Coaching skills
■ Staff are encouraged to ask questions, seek clarification and make comments at appropriate stages of their induction	■ Observation ■ Trainee feedback	■ Interpersonal skills ■ Questioning techniques
■ The training needs of staff are reviewed on a regular and timely basis and appropriate action agreed and implemented to develop them to the standards of performance required	■ Personal development plans ■ Minutes of team staff meetings	■ Application of personal development plans ■ Performance standards
■ Individuals are given accurate evidence and feedback on their achievement of expected levels of performance	■ Appraisal records	■ Appraisal skills
■ Training records are kept up to date, complete and accurate	■ Staff training cards	■ Training database
■ Your own development needs are reviewed on a regular basis with an appropriate authority and action agreed and implemented to help you achieve the desired standards of performance	■ Own personal development plan ■ Minutes of senior team meetings ■ Own appraisal records – both formal and informal	■ Own performance standards ■ Training resources and methods

Appendix 3
An empowerment audit

Rating	What it looks like
A	**Leaders** clarify the vision with the team and individuals, and agree the expectations of their roles, offering support as and when needed.
	Followers have clearly defined expectations for their role and have the skills, knowledge and confidence to carry them out without fear of retribution or interference.
	Systems employ outcomes-focused job profiles from recruitment through to appraisal, and have been in place for three years.
	Development needs are identified by jobholders as well as by the leader, using 360° feedback referring to expressed standards.
	Tools and resources are made available or access is readily approved without undue delay.
B	**Leaders** involve the team in the thinking and planning but closely supervise actions taken.
	Followers feel they have autonomy in their own role but are still subjected to interference from the leader.
	Systems employ job descriptions that sit alongside a 'competency framework' where subjectivity still impedes agreement on performance levels.
	Development needs are identified once a year by leaders for appraisals and action on them depends on time and budget constraints.
	Tools and resources are made available subject to approval and authorisation of a Purchasing Department or other third party.

Rating	What it looks like (cont'd)
C	**Leaders** look ahead and plan to some degree, though in isolation from the team.
	Followers are able to plan to some degree but still have to defend and justify their actions.
	Systems employ basic job descriptions but are seldom referred to after recruitment.
	Development is provided irrespective of a person's experience or ability.
	Tools and resources are identified but available in short supply and not accessible to everyone needing them.
D	**Leaders** react and dictate, making it up as they go along.
	Followers do as they are told, until they get fed up and leave.
	Systems are not employed for describing job roles.
	Development is filed in the out tray – you're out if you can't deliver.
	Tools and resources have not been considered and no authority has been delegated to gain access to them.

Appendix 4
Feedback comments

Below is a fuller listing of the comments received during the structured series of programmes referred to on p. 98.

We have 'witch-hunts' called meetings; the purpose of the meetings is to blame someone.

We never get any feedback on the feedback we do give; we give our opinion and it stops dead.

We get asked questions like: 'What's morale like? How are things going?' Perhaps they should come out of their offices more and see for themselves.

Who takes any notice of our reports? Some of us stopped writing them to see if our managers chased for them, and they don't seem to have noticed that they're not submitted any more.

When you raise queries or objections they tell you you're negative.

'Synergy' is a word they use a lot, but it's never explained – a bit like 'empowerment'.

We have 'post-mortems' before a problem is identified or properly resolved.

Senior management asks me what the hell has gone wrong before I even know there's a problem; it's because they're near to the service control.

Our meetings talk about work tasks rather than work relationships.

They often escalate a problem before it's assessed. They run around like headless chickens like when *abc* went down and it was only one screen but they got it all out of proportion.

There's too much CYA (Cover Your Backside)!

They never sell us anything, they just tell.

There are lots of 'Neils' here (a reference to the Melrose 'Empowerment' video).

They analyse the lines of code you've changed: if you've changed loads in three weeks it shows you're inefficient; if you've only done one in three weeks they think you haven't been productive: you can't win.

Sometimes you have to break the rules, but if you do, and resolve the problem, they still chew you out!

We don't know what plans they have for us. They don't consult us. They have a Career Development Panel that is secretive.

Many of us found out about the change to the company in the computer press. This showed a complete lack of respect and people have not forgiven either employer for the way they were treated.

We only have 'drainpipe' communication.

There is a 'black hole' en route to feeding back to management.

They like to see you working late – you don't get on otherwise.

I'll be surprised if my manager shows any interest in what I thought of this programme.

They're always measuring inputs rather than output.

They use Belbin Team Roles but they don't seem to recognise most of them. You're up or you're out.

They don't accept that mistakes do happen.

You can't be as open as you would like – it could be a major CLM.

We're further and further away from seeing the big picture – no single group knows the whole process.

We were given messages from them that we had to put across – we were told what to say and we couldn't question it. We were not allowed to disagree.

A demarcation line was drawn and has not been breached.

We are not valued for what we are or for what we already contribute.

They'd rather spend money on project celebrations without telling us what it's for, than actually tell us that we've done well.

At least people felt valued before ... if they treat us like children it's not very difficult to act like one.

We almost need a new start for both sides to learn to respect each other.

They are only interested in their own accounts, not in their customers'.

They introduce an evaluation process but don't train us how to evaluate properly.

If the management team were here we wouldn't be making these comments because we'd be on our guard.

We were experts too once ... haven't we got something to offer then? ... All we get now is 'you were working outside accepted company conditions'.

They talk 'we' but don't demonstrate it.

We don't believe that there's no one originally on site capable of filling a board position.

There's a blinkered approach that their way is the right way – we've been here twenty years, they've only been here two.

No one has shown interest in my projects or in what I've got to offer.

They pass you in the corridor and just ignore you – you just feel unvalued.

They only mix horizontally, with their own peer group, not vertically.

They invite you to come and talk to them and then they huddle together in their own group so you feel awkward about interrupting.

I've not seen any evidence of empowerment, but plenty of unempowerment.

We rarely, if ever, see senior management walking around, talking to others or to us.

I have never been told when I am doing a good job.

Their offices make it difficult for them to talk to all the staff and for the staff to get to know the bosses.

We see them using the back stairs to avoid having to talk to us.

You don't get a personal approach or an open question, you get a closed question sent via e-mail.

If they spent time planning it would allow for a better job – an extra two days on a deadline could lead to far better results.

They showed us an organisational hierarchy at the presentation, but then implemented something different without telling us why.

It would be nice if they used your name once in a while.

They don't understand a job-based environment – they're used to going in, preparing a report and having someone else implement the detail while they disappear. Now they have to stick to their own decisions, communicate them and follow through.

They're always making changes without explanation – we don't know where we are sometimes.

We get written team briefs as much as six weeks after they've been written.

They don't use appropriate communication media and they're not consistent anyway.

The team brief is delivered in a 'don't think you'll be interested attitude'. It could be made much more local and relevant.

We want to hear warts and all – not just trumpet blowing.

We've heard no more news on the takeover other than the press – they don't even acknowledge their own vacuum. In fact, we haven't heard the official company line on *xyz* yet.

It was great when he brought the choc-ices round and handed them to you personally – you felt valued.

We get lots of 'what' and not enough 'why'.

Bibliography

Applegarth, M. (1991) *How to Take a Training Audit.* London: Kogan Page.

Blanchard, K. and Hersey, P. (1977) *Management of Organizational Behaviour: Utilizing Human Resources.* Englewood Cliffs, NJ: Prentice-Hall.

Charvet, S.R. (1997) *Words That Change Minds,* 2nd edn. Dubuque, IA: Kendall/Hunt Publishers.

Fang, T. (forthcoming) 'From "onion" to "ocean": paradox and change in national cultures.' Paper under revision for special issue of the *International Studies of Management and Organizations.*

Fielder, F.E., Chemers, M.M. and Mahar, L. (1978) *The Leadership Match Concept.* New York: Wiley.

Hanson, P.C. (1973) *The Annual Handbook for Group Facilitators.* San Diego, CA: Pfeiffer.

Hofstede, G. (1983) 'The cultural relativity of organizational practices and theories', *Journal of International Business Studies,* 14 (2): 75–89.

Hosking, D.M. (1988) 'Organizing, leadership and skilful processes', *Journal of Management Studies,* 25 (2): 147–66.

House, R.J. and Shamir, B. (1993) 'Toward the integration of transformation, charismatic and visionary theories', M.M. Chemers and R. Ayman (eds), *Leadership Theory and Research Perspectives and Directions.* New York: Academic Press, pp. 81–107.

Kübler-Ross, Elisabeth (1969) *On Death and Dying*. New York: Simon & Schuster/Touchstone.

Leavy, B. and Wilson, D.C. (1994) *Strategy and Leadership*. London: Routledge.

Shamir, B., House, R.J. and Arthur, M.B. (1993) 'The motivational effects of charismatic leadership: a self-concept based theory', *Organization Science*, November: 577–94.

Vroom, V.H. and Yetton, P. (1973) *Leadership and Decision Making*. Pittsburgh, PA: University of Pittsburgh Press.

Recommended reading

Posner, K. and Applegarth, M. (1998) *The Project Management Pocketbook*. Alresford, Hants: Management Pocketbooks.

Rosenfeld, R.H. and Wilson, D.C. (1999) *Managing Organizations*, 2nd edn. London: McGraw-Hill.

Index

Printed in the United Kingdom
by Lightning Source UK Ltd.
110330UKS00001BA/13

9 781843 341437